ELEVEN TABLES

A WILD RIDE THROUGH FOOD, FAILURE, AND FIGURING IT OUT

JAMIE A. BROWN

WITH JEFF TONIDANDEL

GREENLEAF
BOOK GROUP PRESS

The recipes in this book have been tested in our kitchens, but results may be different in yours. Always check that food is fully cooked and safe to eat. People with food allergies should read all ingredient lists with care.

Published by Greenleaf Book Group Press
Austin, Texas
www.gbgpress.com

Distributed by Greenleaf Book Group

For ordering information or special discounts for bulk purchases, please contact Greenleaf Book Group at PO Box 91869, Austin, TX 78709, 512.891.6100.

Design and composition by Greenleaf Book Group and Mimi Bark
Cover design by Greenleaf Book Group and Mimi Bark
Cover photography by Jessica Gaddy

Publisher's Cataloging-in-Publication data is available.

Print ISBN: 979-8-88645-422-2

eBook ISBN: 979-8-88645-423-9

To offset the number of trees consumed in the printing of our books, Greenleaf donates a portion of the proceeds from each printing to the Arbor Day Foundation. Greenleaf Book Group has replaced over 50,000 trees since 2007.

Printed in the United States of America on acid-free paper

25 26 27 28 29 30 31 32   10 9 8 7 6 5 4 3 2 1

First Edition

CONTENTS

INTRODUCTION

I shouldn't have been surprised—it was all we'd talked about for months, but people talk crazy when they're on trips; they do adventurous things, and they talk adventurous talk. My husband, Jeff, and I had been in far-off lands, a series of dream worlds—nothing reflecting reality. And yet, there we were, talking about white walls, candles in the windows, and French-inspired menu items: carafes of wine, powdered sugar sprinkled like snow across dessert crêpes, after-dinner coffee as an invitation for guests to stay a while. The idea was romantic, and it had seemed fun to me, too, when we were overseas. But once back home and under pressure (self-imposed as it may have been) to keep up, to save, to someday start a family, Jeff's hopeful statement hit me as an unsettling surprise:

"I want to open that restaurant."

The plan I'd had in mind was different. My husband would be our breadwinner while I worked part-time and had a baby. Life would be comfortable, work would be flexible, and I'd have plenty of time to care for our family at home. Owning a restaurant meant struggle, and I foresaw years of financial uncertainty—watching as everyone else was flourishing while we got by with the income from a small restaurant. I wasn't wrong.

Opening any business comes with huge risk, particularly when it's a business you know nothing about. For Jeff to pursue the restaurant dream, I would need to head back to the corporate universe, get a rigorous job with insurance, and earn a healthy paycheck.

This decision needed my blessing, and I couldn't bring myself to say yes.

Yet, my heart wouldn't let me say no either.

THE BUSINESS OF BELIEF

Looking at me, you might not think: *She must be in restaurants*. I wouldn't blame you; it's not the career I imagined for myself either. With a master of business administration degree in my pocket and my eyes on a career in brand management, I was hungry to absorb anything to do with white-collar crime, tech-industry case studies, financial models, and branding strategies. The restaurant business—with its proverbial full-sleeve tattoos, rugged language, cigarette breaks, and late-night prowling—was never on my short list of career options. Yet, for Jeff and me, it has been the perfect puzzle piece on our journey to building a burgeoning family business.

In 2009, Jeff and I opened our first restaurant in Charlotte, North Carolina, with just eleven tables. Over the past fifteen years, our business has grown by an average of 25 percent each year. We now seat approximately eight thousand people a week at our portfolio of six restaurants, and in 2022, our restaurant Supperland was named one of *Bon Appétit's* Top 10 Best New Restaurants in the country and the #15 Best New Restaurant by *Esquire*. Another of our restaurants, Ever Andalo, was selected by Yelp as the #8 Best New Restaurant in the country—and that was determined by guest reviews and ratings. By mid-2025, we'll have successfully launched three from-scratch restaurant concepts in four years, each of them single-location spots. On top of owning and operating our restaurants, you'll find us on the PBS series *Fork & Hammer*.

Our starting point was unusual: In the midst of the 2009 recession, with no industry knowledge, no experience, and few resources, we blindly jumped into business and opened a restaurant. Since then, the world has changed exponentially and with jaw-dropping speed, and our restaurants, like every business, have been navigating the dynamics of this new world.

Over time, we've tapped into success in a notoriously volatile field, and there are myriad reasons for it. Some of our success has been intentional, some of it borderline accidental, and some of it sheer good fortune. Yet, the most impactful drivers in our evolving journey may not be what you'd expect. Sure, much of our success can be attributed to the careful calculation of figures. But it's thanks in equal balance to the "softer side" of business, those elements that might be casually overlooked as insignificant but which play leading roles in achieving success.

I'm here to tell you that not only do the little things matter, but they've made the difference between a single-location, eleven-table restaurant and a developing restaurant group aimed at destination-worthy dining experiences. There's no special sauce, but if I had to put my finger on the secret ingredient that threads through everything, it's belief.

Belief is the spark, the genesis, the starting point before something intangible comes to be. Belief is what we had before we earned confidence from our successes—because belief is seeing that which doesn't yet exist—and that tiny light of belief opens up a world of possibility and creation.

WHAT'S ON THE BOOK MENU

I've heard people say you have to earn confidence. Ours surely swelled when we saw the results of hard work, unusual vision, teamwork, creativity, and loving leadership. But confidence is not the same thing as belief. So much of our success has come down to having a vision and believing that the pieces would come together before that confidence arrived. It takes belief to begin, to start anything new—especially when it means letting go of what we've created to start all over again.

Jeff and I believe in our dream and in each other. We believe in our concepts, our menus, and our teammates. We believe that restaurants build community and inspire people. We believe in bigger things for ourselves. And we believe in bigger things for every individual out there. We've witnessed belief, combined with all the other ancillary ingredients that make our business model work, and we're all about sharing those family recipes. But before we begin, here's a broad look at our restaurant concepts in order of opening so you can more easily follow along in the stories to come.

Crêpe Cellar opens — 2009
Growlers Pourhouse opens — 2010
Haberdish opens — 2016
Reigning Doughnuts opens — 2017
Supperland opens — 2021
Ever Andalo replaces Crêpe Cellar — 2021
Leluia Hall opens — 2022
2025

Someday . . . we open the historic Leeper-Wyatt concept and our company's commissary kitchen.

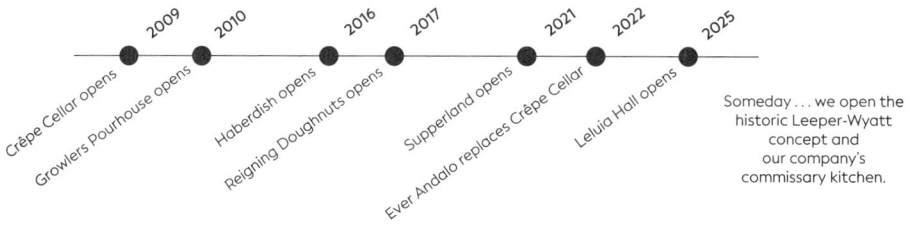

Crêpe Cellar—This was our first restaurant, and we opened in the bottom of the recession in April 2009 in the NoDa (formerly North Davidson) neighborhood of Charlotte. It was a gastropub serving savory and sweet crêpes. We closed this business in 2022 to open an Italian spot, Ever Andalo, in its place.

Growlers Pourhouse—Our craft beer bar with just fourteen taps that sits next door to the Crêpe Cellar space on the busy corner of Thirty-Fifth and North Davidson. It opened in August 2010 and shares a kitchen with our restaurant next door.

Haberdish—Here we serve up fried chicken and cocktails, all meant to dive into Charlotte's food history. It's also in NoDa, a couple doors down from our other concepts in that neighborhood.

Reigning Doughnuts—We transformed a back closet space in 2017 at Growlers Pourhouse and converted it into a walk-up window for hot, fresh, made-to-order doughnuts. We have no space inside—it's eighty-two square feet in there—just enough room for a couple workers, coffee, and a doughnut machine.

Supperland—We opened this large dining hall-esque restaurant on the tail end of the pandemic in 2021. It is a grand space—a former mid-century church—with two buildings. As a "steakhouse meets church potluck" menu, along with our family style dining, it flips the idea of a steakhouse on its head. We uniquely have a speakeasy on the basement floor of our bar building too.

Ever Andalo—This restaurant concept has replaced Crêpe Cellar as of March 2022. It is a buzzy Italian spot and an ode to Jeff's family name, Tonidandel—a family history that originates in the Dolomites of Italy.

Leluia Hall—Like Supperland, this concept is also in a former church. But this church is in the historic Dilworth neighborhood of Charlotte, and it's a 1915 structure that has needed a lot of work. Inside its doors, we serve a steak and surf menu, all family style, with a bright, fresh flavor profile.

Leeper-Wyatt building (forthcoming)—This concept isn't named yet, but this is the historic landmark building that we physically moved 750 feet to save from demolition. It will be its own restaurant concept someday, and it sits next to Leluia Hall in Dilworth.

Commissary Kitchen (forthcoming)—This commissary kitchen will provide a spot for our team to bake breads, make homemade pastries and pastas, do butchery, whip up cocktail syrups, and cook stocks and broths for our whole restaurant group. This concept is not named or created yet, but it is located in a rather ugly flat-top industrial building in South End Charlotte.

Other projects—I don't know yet, but we stay open to the idea.

In this book, you'll find a chapter-by-chapter breakdown of the most important elements we've found in building a thriving heart-led business, all woven with the stories that have gotten us here. On the journey, you'll discover how to see more for yourself, step boldly into an exciting dream life, create with intention, persist through difficulties, trust others to help in the process, be open to change as you go, manage the risks that come with any business venture, and then—like a large virtuous cycle—further build upon the all-important belief that started it all.

One

SEE MORE FOR YOURSELF

Go from good to great with a garnish.

When was the last time you thought about what you really wanted? Imagined the possibilities behind "what if"? Allowed your mind to take you on flights of fancy through different realities? Took a big bite of your own potential?

As a young girl, I saw myself floating in space as an astronaut or picking through the mouth of a stranger in dentistry. I never dreamed about restaurants. Yet, in my youth, Saturday afternoons were best spent with my siblings turning our dining room table into our own eatery.

At each place setting, we would set a copy of a crayon-colored menu with options like peanut butter and jelly, cheese and crackers, or grapes. The eats were subpar, but it was sheer joy to create a menu, take people's orders, serve the food, and provide for our guests—usually my rather patient mother and a younger sibling who was just happy to get attention. I came from a conservative Christian home with a lot of mouths to feed, so we didn't eat out much. Restaurants were fantasies, perfect for pretend play.

When my siblings and I were young, we ate like everyone else in the late seventies and early eighties. Brightly colored commercial foods matched the fashion trends rising around us: sugary cereals and slushy drinks, sweet toaster tarts, and flashy potato chip bags. But around 1982, my dad radically changed his diet—and the rest of the family diet along with it. After this, we were raised on a macrobiotics meal plan: sautéed kale and seaweed—quite rare in Pittsburgh at the time—and common veggies, like broccoli, brussels sprouts, green beans, carrots, and peas. Our grains were whole: brown rice, amaranth, quinoa, and millet. We had some fish and chicken, and lots of legumes, like adzuki beans, lentils, and kidney beans. Red meat was a rare treat, relegated to the occasional burger on a "fun" night. Those celebratory bags of artificially flavored and preserved corn chips disappeared.

When the family diet changed, the joy I got from eating plummeted. Dinner was something to get through, not enjoy. Meals were more about ingesting bites, cleaning it up, packing a leftover lunch, and doing it all over again the next day. My mom had nine mouths to feed, and the job needed to get done. She did it with grace, day after day—and often without gratitude from us kids. I loved other people's food, whether at friends' houses, at restaurants, or at my grandmother Malu Audrey's home. So when I was old enough, the first job I applied for during high school was at a restaurant. I didn't get the job as a table busser (I forgot a pen!), but I never lost my admiration for people in the hospitality industry.

Something subtle, quiet, was luring me toward food. And just two hours away, a little boy named Jeff was also unknowingly being led in the same direction.

At Jeff's house in Cleveland, Ohio, the food was very Stouffer's-centric: Stouffer's lasagna, Stouffer's Welsh rarebit, Stouffer's turkey tetrazzini, and Stouffer's chipped beef. When his mom did cook, Jeff watched her over-boil pasta or microwave cheese on bread with the expected results. His family belonged to a tennis and skating club, and for special occasions like birthdays or holidays, they'd enjoy a buffet-style meal of soups, roast beef, salads, and seafood bisques. Jeff wanted to learn a better way, so he began to cook. At first, it was simple things like grilled cheese sandwiches and different styles of eggs. Then, he graduated to recipes from cooking shows like *Yan Can Cook*. He dug up cookbooks and made the recipes to the letter. There was a difference in how food was prepared outside his home, and Jeff craved to understand why.

After Jeff's parents split, food was different in his father's home. "Pops," as we came to call Jeff's dad, was a vegetarian, and—like my dad—he was big on whole grains. Pops did his food shopping at hippie health-food stores, which were usually located in dingy, low-rent neighborhoods, where he found ingredients like aloe vera juice, tofu, ancient-grain bread, and walls of vitamins.

The first handful of times Jeff stayed with his dad in his new apartment, his father put hours of effort into cooking and cleaning for his growing boys. It was unsustainable. Eventually, he simplified and cut out reviews from the daily paper, which inspired dinner destinations, both local and more adventurous. Cleveland had plenty of Italian places—the Tonidandels' heritage was one of breads and pastas—but the family also frequented Johnny Mango for Caribbean fried plantains with pico de gallo or drove to Tommy's in Coventry for falafel sandwiches. When the boys traveled for tennis matches, Pops stowed newspaper reviews for eating spots at their destination. The joy of tasting the new, discovering flavorful combinations and interesting textures, and putting ingredients together to savory and delicious ends stayed with Jeff through college and beyond.

While food played a role in our upbringings, our childhood relationships to food aren't the reason for our career path. Neither of us had been encouraged into the kitchen, nor were we nudged by the existence of former family businesses. It's a wonder we ended up where we are—except we had both gotten in the habit of following our hearts.

When my father thought I was crazy for going to grad school in Los Angeles, I went anyway. When I took a lower-paying marketing job at Lance over a high-paying tech job at Lowe's Home Improvement, I did it because the job sounded more fun. When Jeff and I quit our jobs, stuffed our belongings in storage, and traveled around Europe, everyone thought we were insane. We did it because we wanted to.

Freedom from the obligation to do what others expected was something I somehow garnered early in life, and I married a man who shared that same mentality. So it's no surprise, really, that we took "what if?" and ran with it.

CRACKERS AND CARS

Before our restaurant days, as newlyweds, we were just-minted MBAs. It was the early 2000s, and we landed pretty solid corporate gigs. On the thin but busy strip of South Boulevard at the company then known as Lance Snack Foods, I was groomed for branding and product management. Lance made ToastChee, the bright orange cheese sandwich crackers filled with peanut butter, which outsold any other product we had by sevenfold at the time, as well as jerkies and nuts, snack mixes, Gold-n-Chees crackers, and Cape Cod Potato Chips, many of which were made onsite. The mix of packaging design, web development, product testing, and merchandising my job required amounted to a weird kind of career heaven.

In the first production room I could get to from my office, orange square crackers slowly streamed out of the wide ovens, thousands of them in skinny rows. At the far end of the line, I watched a lady pore over those crackers like a foreman, pulling any that were too dark or that had crinkled or crumpled on the journey. The culled crackers were tossed in a round gray trash bin with all the other imperfect bits. From that point on the assembly line, I made my way backward down the line as the crackers became less package-worthy as long flat sheets, uncut and uncooked. I looked up through a chute to where the dough came from, the mixing room one floor up, snaked my way upstairs, and pushed open the bakery door.

A waft of tangy air hit my nose—the yeast, rising from gigantic vats of dough, pillowed upward. Steps away, I slid inside another closed door, where it was warmer and the steam of yeast grew and thickened the air.

Huge four-foot-high tubs held batter as it rose, readying it for baking. Around the corner, a machine affixed to the back of a vat lifted the dough over a chute. Slowly, the machine tilted toward the chute, and a ball of dough the size of a small car tumbled inward and downward to flatten out. Perhaps I should have known back then that the food industry was where I belonged; I could have watched that dough all day.

While I was playing with snack foods, Jeff had found a unique career in hospitality—managing sponsorships for NASCAR's team, then known as Chip Ganassi Racing with Felix Sabates. Thirty-eight weeks of the year, he flew all over the country, entertaining clients, schmoozing, and doing anything to make track visits more pleasant for his guests. Team sponsors attended the races, often with VIPs and spokespeople, and Jeff showed them all a good time, even picking them up in golf carts and toting them around the pits for close-up views of the brightly colored cars stickered with company names.

It was the heyday of NASCAR, and after a day at the racetrack, Jeff arranged dinners for a dozen people chummed up around a large table, sharing stories, imbibing craft cocktails, and treating themselves to the best champagnes a corporate card could buy. There was an inherent art to Jeff's job; salesmanship and relationship-building required genuine care for people, resulting in sales worth millions of dollars. The sponsors allowed the team to keep racing, and the hospitality they were shown, in great part, kept them sponsoring. Simply put, Jeff was good at it. But it wasn't the glitz and glamour that he loved. It was caring for people.

At home, Jeff turned his attention to me: Reservations, trips, dinners out, and dinners in brought sparks of joy to our lives. He was a curator of sorts, and I benefited from his whims: private flights, Sonoma wineries, and sleeping under the stars by a Carolina lake. Jeff loved a good time, but more than that—more than anything—he loved to show others a good time.

All that love of curating was about to get its first ride as we tinkered our way toward a path of creating, owning, and operating restaurants.

YEARNING FOR A NEW FLAVOR

Even as Jeff and I were blooming in the kinds of corporate careers we'd dreamed of, our hearts yearned for something else. I envisioned a more worldly version of myself, one I wouldn't find in my comfortable Southern city; plus, I was feeling pulled to write. Jeff was simultaneously soul-searching. We knew there would be something else out there . . . if we only took the time to seek it. We wanted to *go places*.

I didn't come from a family of travelers. My childhood vacations were mainly road trips, my parents schlepping us kids from our hometown of Pittsburgh to Atlanta or the Jersey Shore. Jeff didn't do much traveling as a kid either, except when his father was playing in tennis tournaments, and they camped in their van at sites near the courts. Traveling hadn't shaped who we were, but Jeff and I dreamed that travel would be a part of who we'd become.

We were young and unafraid, so we took the gamble, quit our well-paying corporate jobs, sold or gave away what we could, boxed up our other belongings, and packed our studio apartment into a small storage space. We left behind those crackers and cars—strong careers with massive potential—attended goodbye parties, and tended to comments from all the rational, intelligent people who gave us an earful about us neglecting responsibility. But our minds were certain: Our life was going to be different, kicked off by one brazen decision to travel.

It was 2007, and as the days counted down to our trip away, our back-packs arrived, along with quick-dry towels, sturdy water bottles, passport holders that hung around our necks, and a small first aid kit. Jeff packed and repacked our camera gear, travel books, maps, and computer equipment a half dozen times. Newlyweds for just a year, we were ready to begin our new nomadic lifestyle.

Surely while we were gone, we'd pick up clues for what to do when we came back home.

FROM EXPLORATION TO INSPIRATION

To this day, Jeff and I have found one of the best ways for us to grow and learn is by noting, respecting, and admiring the intricacies of the world around us. Visiting and experiencing places around the world—whether directly related to hospitality or not—is just a part of what Jeff and I do. That notion began with us packing up to go see the world. We didn't have a plan; we just went one day at a time.

To start, in April that year, Jeff and I made our way to El Salvador for two weeks with Habitat for Humanity to build a house in a remote town near the border of Guatemala. Block by block, we built around rebar, slopped mortar into place, and scraped it back for neatness. During breaks, wrinkled old ladies emerged from their homes carrying trays laden with rich golden mangoes from nearby trees and colorful arrays of Gatorade.

We ate beans and arepas for breakfast, and often for dinner too. Jeff and I stayed with our team in a single-story motel where our shower didn't drain and the overhead shower stream sent tingling shocks to your back. It was electrically heated water and, apparently, broken. We stomped cockroaches and shooed lizards out the door, and learned to shower, as much as we could, in the sink. When our trip to El Salvador ended, I looked down at my forearms, browned from long days in the sun and now draped with bright string bracelets I had purchased from barefooted children. I liked how my skin looked—my hands had been used, and used for good.

Shortly after our return from El Salvador, Jeff and I took a one-way flight to London with a simple plan: We'd take every day as it came, making arrangements as we went. If we enjoyed a place, we'd stay longer. If the sun rose and we felt ready to move on, we would. It was a bizarre exercise in freedom—except that we had a finite amount of money to spend and no plan for return.

Hostels accommodated our price point, as did small apartments with lower negotiated rents for extended visits. Shared bathrooms meant cheaper stays, and sleeping on trains or boats overnight also kept costs down. We visited museums on free and discounted days. One backpack served as a repository for complimentary packaged crackers and leftover napkin-wrapped baguettes after a dinner out. A jar of peanut butter, along with a couple overused plastic forks, was slid snuggly in a side pocket to smear on those free carbs we collected.

From Florence to Madrid to Prague to Kyoto, our steps across the wide world grew, and tiny, unknown-to-us towns became familiar, now-bright spots in our past. In each new spot, our plates were filled with ingredients and dishes that had never crossed our lips—tastes and combinations and manners of cooking we had never experienced.

Without a home kitchen, we ate from the kitchens and markets of the world. Our eyes opened, hungry to learn, now seeing the world through the lens of food.

In London, we gathered with old friends to feast around steak and frites. On plates thick and round, hearty piles of steak and potatoes were bathed in a demi-glace that pooled at the bottom of the plate. We stayed mere days, though; the unfavorable exchange rate to the pound sent Jeff and me scurrying out of London and on to Italy.

For a week, we rested our heads in a monastery atop the plateau of Volterra, with vast lookouts in every direction over the wide Italian country-side below. Most of our time was spent outside the silent monastery—with chunky cherub heads always peering down at us—preferring the busy alleyways of the winding Italian town. I could hardly get enough of my new favorite pizza, the girasole (with tomatoes, eggplant, and mozzarella), or piles of fresh pasta and half carafes of local wine.

We twisted down the backstreets of Siena to duck into an Italian restaurant—white curtains flowed in the breeze as we cut into a tightly layered vegetarian lasagna with fresh pasta, ricotta, squash, spinach, and herbs.

Sometimes on our travels we had a small kitchen, as we did in our quirky split-room apartment in the Dolomites of northern Italy. Floating above wine country, our bedroom was on the left side of the public hallway, and our kitchen and bathroom were across the hall on the right. The smell of buttery pasta filled the small, yellowed kitchenette with dumpling-esque homemade spaetzle—which we learned to make from new Italian friends—boiled and sautéed until it was brown and the little corners got all crispy.

A distant relative of Jeff's introduced us to grappa, a hard liquor made from grape skins that he kept nestled in a jacket pocket, ready to swig at all times or be poured into pop, juice, tea, or his favorite, coffee—calling it "cafe correcto." With the grappa, Jeff's newly discovered distant family served large trays of sheet-pan polenta, sliced like bread loaves, with stewed beef and long noodles. Our new Italian friends whisked us away one night to a remote cabin in the woods, an eight-table restaurant serving food from the land, like pig's feet, truffles, and venison.

We foraged for mushrooms in the wet soil of the Dolomites, searching for the perfect fungi and finding none because all the elderly gentlemen had been out trolling hours before, checking the secret spots where the fungus grew. We collected free lemons from the ground in Sorrento, using them to freshen up our lukewarm tap water bottles.

We learned how strange it was (apparently) to put fruit on one's plate for dinner—the fruit was meant to be enjoyed after dinner. We also learned that Italians don't all make homemade pasta and sauce; they enjoy the convenience of Barilla boxed pastas as well. When our Italian friends met us in Barcelona, where we shared an apartment with a kitchen, we learned that some Europeans have no idea how to work a microwave. They tried to dry the silverware in the microwave box, thinking the heat would evaporate the water, and sparks flew inside the cooker like the Fourth of July.

We squeezed sideways to fit at a table in a tiny French crêperie, discovering the beautiful concept of enjoying a half carafe of wine and street crêpes in the middle of the day. There was nothing like that back home in Charlotte—crêpes that felt elegant enough to enjoy at dinnertime with wine, that made you feel like you had stepped away from the norm and transported yourself somewhere beautiful and romantic, somewhere like the busy streets of Paris.

In San Sebastián, Spain, there was no treating ourselves to the numerous expensive Michelin-starred restaurants, so we frequented the market and the narrow counters of *pinxtos* bars. In Granada, we wandered la Alhambra in sheer awe and spent an evening in a cave-like room in the slope of a hillside, watching spirited flamenco dancers steal the room with their abrupt gestures and animated faces. For six weeks, we hunkered in an apartment in the wall of Tarifa, with easy access to meander the streets and enjoy time and coffee in the open windows of a whitewashed stone building, watching the golden flickers of candles sprinkled across the sill.

Bordeaux enticed a visit with a long-lost cousin, Kelly, and her husband, Oliver, who lived in a small home with a backyard stretching along rows of vines belonging to their neighbor's vineyard. I still recall their child's abrupt critique of a stale baguette that was brought home one morning. "Daddy," she said in a lovely French accent, "this baguette is no good." He got back in his car and immediately returned the baguette to the shop.

In Seoul, South Korea, we met up with my adopted brothers from Korea who had moved back "home" after spending their childhoods with our family in Pittsburgh. We took a day to visit their birth mother and grandmother in a small apartment outside of Seoul. Large cylindrical tubs of cabbage, sliced thin, sat fermenting in their living room. We walked to the nearby market where several blocks alongside the river were tented with merchants selling from tables heaped with seafood, all the fresh blues and pinks and yellows of creatures just pulled up from the sea. Just-chopped octopus tentacles crawled with life up wooden chopsticks after being butchered and dashed with hot sauce. We learned the etiquette for serving alcohol in Korea—always poured by others, not yourself, and always served with a second hand holding or at least touching the bottle.

One day we entered a gorgeous Japanese garden in Kyoto where pristine flowers sprang up from meticulously crafted mounds of dirt surrounding a Michelin-starred restaurant. We could only afford their discounted breakfast, but what arrived in front of us were the most neatly manicured bowls of rice with an egg on top, petite like a quail egg and perfectly orange and plump. Beside the egg were delicate stacks of purple, pink, and yellow pickled daikon, cabbage, and radish. Another day we found a restaurant with on-floor dining. We crouched on narrow mats, sitting on our bottoms to enjoy noodles and broth. Jeff needed a block, or a back rest, or . . . a chair—as his knees lingered up toward his shoulders in discomfort while he slurped.

Surrounded by looming trees, we meandered miles into the mountains to stay in a Buddhist temple, eating tofu and seaweed for breakfast. And lunch. And dinner, with hot bitter tea alongside. After two days of eating vegan on the bamboo floors of our bedroom at the temple, we gorged on large slices of pepperoni pizza in a dark restaurant at the base of the mountain.

After macrobiotic cooking in my childhood and four years of living off dining hall food and cans of beefaroni in college, it was a gobsmacking culture shock to ingest the dizzying variety and nuances of food springing forth from every corner of the world. And for hours, with little else to occupy us, Jeff and I fell into dreamy conversations, sparking moments of utter bliss imagining our future together. As we wandered, without intent, our words more and more appeared to be floating wistfully in a new direction . . . of us someday opening a restaurant.

What kind of food would we serve? What would it look like? How would we serve different dishes? What would we call it? How could we make it truly special? The brainstorming was continuous—a flood of ideas loosely captured but ever growing and ever building.

After eight months living out of backpacks and roaming the wide expanses of Europe and Asia, we made the difficult decision to head home. Our plane landed back in Pittsburgh, and a few hours later, I knelt next to my grandmother's bed and held her hand—an eighty-six-year-old hand that had held mine so many times. I told Malu Audrey that we'd made it back, that our trip was amazing, that we got to see so many things, that I missed her, that I loved her. Her room was lined with people—all of us who used to gather to celebrate holidays around tables filled with food prepared by this now-frail woman, lying in her bed.

Memories flashed: warm homemade lemon cookies stowed two to a bag. Her fridge stocked with pop we'd never be allowed to have at home. The beef stew she brought to the house when my parents had to go out of town. Sunday snacks of crackers and spray-on cheese or strawberries coated in powdered sugar. Sleepovers with just us girls. Studying at her house for grad school standard tests. Christmas morning when she'd come to our house with still more gifts—all wrapped crisply from corner to corner with thick wrapping paper and pristine bows. Even the phone calls I had been making from pay phones across Europe to hear her voice.

Malu passed the day after we arrived home.

It was time for us to be back. Life was calling us home to do something. Yet it was with no small amount of embarrassment that we realized, despite having spent all those months seeking and soul-searching, we had no greater understanding of what.

IMPACTFUL MOVES

What it was about the Carolinas that called us back, I'm not sure. Maybe it was that we'd lived there before our trip, so we knew what to expect. Maybe we thought we'd have an easier time finding jobs. Maybe we returned because all our belongings were locked in a storage room three miles outside the city of Charlotte. In hindsight, returning to the Carolinas was probably the path of least resistance, but the path seemed to lead somewhere, even though Jeff and I were unaware of the direction we were heading. When a family member offered up their small lake house in Albemarle, North Carolina, for the winter to help us get settled, we took the opportunity.

Our new bedroom barely fit two small single beds covered in light blue terry cloth bedspreads. We had grown accustomed to sleeping in separate beds on our travels—the norm in hostels—but the quiet space left us feeling empty, so we pushed the beds together to lessen the melancholy of the cold January, silent and lifeless.

The end of 2007 was the beginning of the recession, and jobs in Charlotte were hard to come by. I snagged the first opportunity that came my way: retail at lululemon. The company was opening a showroom in Charlotte to build a grassroots following before opening a full-scale store. With employment, however modest, Jeff and I found an itty-bitty studio apartment near the city, and Jeff got on the tennis court to teach lessons (he'd played in college and even served as the Davidson College assistant women's tennis team coach for a couple years). That would help tide us over until he found the kind of work he said he wanted, in the newly expanding field of "green" development and city planning.

A handful of weeks into our new routine, Jeff took me out to dinner. Over pizza and a hefeweizen, we had the conversation that would change our lives—the one about opening that restaurant we had so wistfully dreamed of. It was a once-beautiful idea that suddenly felt incredibly frightening. I couldn't say no, but I didn't want to say yes.

Over the months that followed, I slowly slid into a support role. My heart wasn't sold on the plan, but if this was actually a possibility, I didn't want it to wreck us financially. With Jeff hellbent on opening a restaurant, at the very least I could contribute my skill set: I could help with a marketing plan, a branding plan, a business plan. That was as big of a yes as I could muster.

In 2008, all around us, people were losing their jobs or afraid of losing their jobs. The stock market was tanking and uncertainty loomed. And there I was typing up a business plan to send to family and friends in pursuit of investors for our first restaurant. Our colorful business plan was complete with restaurant stats and Charlotte growth figures, and inspirational food and decor photos to help articulate our vision for a new dining place. Jeff attached a financial model of anticipated revenue, food costs, and labor costs.

Hurdling over a mountain of self-doubt, we sent it out. The email hit inboxes of parents, siblings, cousins, good friends, and former business school pals. We tried to keep our expectations in check, but we couldn't help hoping someone might say yes.

It didn't take long for the "no thanks" emails, notes, and calls to start flooding back.

People thought we were naïve, that we were unequipped to open a restaurant—physically, mentally, and experience-wise. They weren't wrong. We had never owned or operated any business, let alone a restaurant. Neither of us had gone to culinary school, or even worked one day as a server, busser, food runner, or any type of kitchen staff. Plus, it was a recession.

With noes mounting up, we continued to send out our plan. Then, after a few months, Jeff had a surprising call with a childhood friend named Charles, who, having done extraordinarily well with his hedge fund in New York City, was interested in learning more. He committed as our primary investor, footing the bill for the majority of our first buildout. Charles had no restaurant experience, but he wanted to diversify his investments, and he had cash to loan. Knocking on enough doors had paid off—one eventually creaked open and, rather than shutting us out, the person on the other side held the ticket for us to venture forward.

Forward we went as novices, with so much to learn.

See, we didn't know it then, but restaurants don't just sell food. They sell happiness, good feelings, conversation pieces, memories, experiences, warm hospitality, leisure, and everything in between. Each guest walks into our building and becomes a part of the collective, borderline-theatrical experience in which the restaurant is the setting and the guests are both actors and the audience. At our restaurants, Jeff and I sell a whole vibe, yet we're not the people on the front line selling.

Our team—servers, bartenders, hosts, managers, and kitchen staff—performs the orchestration every night. That has taken a lot of trust. With that requirement of trust, Jeff and I have learned to be measured and detailed in setting up our business frameworks with strong leaders, richness, stories, and guardrails that keep focus on consistently great service and food quality every night our doors are open.

We now live in a beautiful world teeming with vibrance—and all the good and tough things that come along with that. Intermeshed, there's beautiful food, animated people, new ideas, blissful moments, gigantic risk, joy and savoring, obstacles of all kinds, and one-of-a-kind creation. And none of it would have been possible without a few yeses—no matter how quiet some of them were.

SERVING SPOON: There's something in you that wants to come to life. It needs a yes. You're the only one who can bring it about. What is that thing?

Two

STEP IN BOLDLY

Crack eggs with confidence.

Our foundation to get started in restaurants was that overseas trip we took and all the intricacies of what we learned and captured along the way—but the bigger feat was the act of listening to our hearts and then actually doing something about it. That stepping forward boldly into something new despite not having answers, that was the true miracle. And that manner of living is now threaded in all we do.

It sounds like we always had it figured out. We didn't. Our leap into restaurants was far from perfect, far from intentional. I wasn't confident it would all work out—it's one of the riskiest and most volatile businesses around. It's only in hindsight that I see how critical those early steps were. They were bold, yes. But they were also flooded with uncertainty.

One night in our early days of opening restaurants, I sat awake in my bed thinking of the walled town of Tarifa, Spain, where Jeff and I had spent six weeks nestled in a single-room apartment built into the tall stone walls surrounding the city. Down a tight alleyway just wide enough for a

Fiat and through an open atrium, our door was a thick wooden hunk with a metal overlay. A gigantic knocking mechanism studded the front, and a hinge stuck and creaked when the door opened. On Tarifa evenings, we'd bounce from one café to another, watching flamenco dancing, enjoying coffee, and sipping cheap sangria. At night, we would pack ourselves into the bottom of a bunk bed, the smell of incense and weed wafting up from the street, snuggled tight in the wall of an ancient city.

In Tarifa, we started writing down thoughts in a little journal we called *Crazy*. Our scribbles included a French-inspired restaurant reminiscent of the streets of France. Savory buckwheat crêpes stacked with colorful garnishes; servers shaking powdered sugar and pouring half carafes of wine for tight budgets; farm-to-table vegetables, minced fresh or roasted or fried; fresh bread with crust that crackled when you pulled it apart. All in a dark, dimly lit room that made you never want to leave. In that journal was written proof: What Jeff and I were doing by opening a restaurant, we had dreamed of doing together.

The reality, though, was different. Even a couple months prior to opening, we weren't working at the restaurant together. I was working at another job and narrowly making it home to see Jeff before he had to leave for work. Our romantic dream had only separated us. I guess it was the "we" part that was amiss. I was in a full support role, working to hold everything together month to month so he could "play" restaurant. I didn't feel resentful of him; I felt proud of his bravery and his start. But our reality together wasn't what I imagined.

Those initial steps into the restaurant business were the best we could do at that time. We stepped. Even in the uncertainty, we marched forward. I didn't know it then, but that was really all we needed to do.

Since we first opened in 2009, interest in food has grown. People care about farming and where ingredients come from. There's nuance to proper dining service. There's heated controversy around chemicals and the ways our food is grown. People want to know what wines pair with food flavor profiles. Cooking at home is in. Eating out is in. Traveling to try restaurants is in. Phrases like *what grows together goes together, the slow food movement, food as medicine*, and the word *foodie* all have become part of our vernacular. People are looking for convenience with food, and they're also seeking experiences.

We didn't know much of this when we got started, but we did know that pouring yourself into something will give you a better shot at making it. Timid steps bring tiny results. So we poured ourselves into it, and we did the bold things, the scary things, the uncertain things—all to get started on a new path.

PUSH THE DOOR OPEN

When Jeff and I first began looking for restaurant spaces in 2008 to open Crêpe Cellar, I went along with him, more out of curiosity than to be genuinely supportive. We had scoured Charlotte for a spot, and with the recession, landlords may have been desperate, but no one was clamoring for inexperienced restaurant tenants.

One day, we were walking through an artsy neighborhood on North Davidson Street, known as NoDa, two miles northeast of Charlotte's center city. The small neighborhood was dotted with independent shops, art galleries, and mom-and-pop restaurants. It was one of the few areas with reasonable restaurant rent rates, so we'd been going there on repeat. As we passed the yellow brick walls of a facade of what had been Fat City, a longtime bar and café, our eyes veered across the street. Hanging on the doorknob of a small restaurant was a notice. We crossed the street for a closer look. The restaurant had not paid its gas bill.

We had eaten there just a few months before. Our table in the middle of the room had been set for four. Open windows lined the front wall, and hot, stagnant air filled the space. A lone fan hovered above, trying its mightiest, but to no avail. The server brought out jerk chicken, plantains, and rice, sweat dripping from his forehead to his arms. The food sang with notes of hearty, meaningful family recipes, but the room was devoid of patrons.

The day we lifted the notice off the doorknob, Jeff called the landlord and got confirmation that the tenant had stopped paying their bills. The owner had skipped town.

Everything happened quickly after that. Just a week later, Jeff came home with a bottle in hand to celebrate. We would be opening an independent restaurant in a neighborhood on the brink of either success or deterioration, in the middle of the worst economic climate in decades, with a bunch of used equipment and no idea how to use any of it. The restaurant would be called Crêpe Cellar Kitchen & Pub, and it would serve up savory and sweet crêpes and other higher-end, homemade pub food.

Piece by piece, our restaurant space began to morph into a quaint European gastropub. Large wooden mirrors hung on the back wall—not just to make the room feel bigger but also because they were cheaper than artwork and many other types of decor. Jeff and I had seen a restaurant in New York write specials on mirrors, and we figured that might work at Crêpe Cellar too. We painted the walls several times, unable to settle on a color we loved—but we ended up with a light blue in the dining room and light yellow in the back hallway. I never loved the colors, but I didn't have the bandwidth to suggest a change. It was truly Jeff's project. I was ancillary, supporting mostly by allowing.

Our bathroom hallway needed more separation from the dining room, so we built a two-thirds wall with a woven wooden framework on top to visually separate the spaces. We purchased eleven butcher-block tabletops and affixed them to the former tenant's sturdy iron table bases. We didn't have a lot of money budgeted for flooring, so we stained the existing floor a shiny brownish color.

Jeff leaned on the expertise of his new business partner, Paul Manley, who had a decade of restaurant experience and was willing to consult on the place and offer ongoing leadership for 10 percent ownership. The two guys drove up to my hometown outside of Pittsburgh to purchase used booths from a well-loved restaurant called Roxy's, which had become a victim of the recession. Jeff bought a portable crêpe griddle, round and slick, to practice making crêpes. It was as heavy as a car engine, but it was electric and could be toted with a little brawn to anywhere that had a plug. Jeff bought several crêpe spinners, too, to see if he preferred wood or metal. And eventually, he had a colleague from his former race team custom-make spinners for our team to use in the Crêpe Cellar kitchen. Finesse is key in making crêpes, especially if you're making hundreds in succession. The batter is watery thin, and you use the spinner to swirl it in a circular motion as it spreads out into a round, papery pancake. The spinner matters a lot.

Jeff practiced at home and in front of small groups, which came from unexpected directions. One time he made crêpes for a twenty-five-person yoga class on a Saturday morning. When Savasana ended, Jeff stood in front of the room to pour batter over the hot, heavy griddle. Guests held bendy paper plates as he served up fresh crêpes with creamy Nutella mixing with perfectly ripe bananas. These baby steps toward our new life weren't perfect, but we weren't aiming for perfection yet. It was about getting even tiny bits of energy moving in the direction of success, about thinking differently, and putting ourselves out there, even if we were tiptoeing at first. Especially me.

BUMPY STARTS ARE STILL STARTS

The December after we signed the lease on the Crêpe Cellar space, I was two months pregnant, still working retail in a shop rumored to be closing because of the recession, and managing a job search in the corporate universe. In the colder, wetter weather, Jeff's tennis lessons had dwindled to near nothing. He was working hard and fast on the restaurant, but the opening was still months away, and we knew enough to understand that even once it did open, we'd have a long road before there was steady money coming in.

One night a couple weeks before Christmas, Jeff giddily took my arm as we were walking up to our apartment. "Close your eyes," he said. I hadn't seen him giddy like that in a while. I closed my eyes.

We turned the corner, and I heard his key turning the lock. "You can look now."

Twinkling lights looped and cascaded up and down the branches of a Christmas tree, nearly seven feet tall, taking up a large corner of our tiny apartment. Beside the tree was the box of ornaments that had come from my recently passed grandmother's storage closet. He had bought a tree stand and a skirt so it could glow in our window overlooking Morehead Street. It was supposed to be beautiful.

"Damn it, Jeff!" I screamed at him, pulling my arm away from his. "Why do you have to do things like this?"

My body fell between my bent knees, my hands on my face. *Rent. No savings. No steady income. Restaurant opening. Gigantic toss-away Christmas tree with sparkling lights. And . . . a baby now on the way.* That was how Christmas felt to me that year. Then the retail shop where I worked closed, and I lost my job.

It wouldn't have taken much to convince Jeff to get a corporate job. He loved me, respected me, and wanted me to have the life of my dreams. But coercion wasn't my style. Even though it wasn't what I'd planned, I knew what I needed to do.

It was early in the morning; I had an interview in two hours. A few months pregnant, I wasn't showing much, but tiny movements fluttered in my belly. I needed this job—the paycheck, the insurance, the stability. I slid a black tank top over my head and pulled out my dark gray pinstriped suit. The zipper stopped three-quarters of the way up, and the button wouldn't fasten. I stepped into a black "belly band" to encircle my waist and cover my unbuttoned pants. At least my jacket buttoned. In my mirror, the woman in front of me stood tall. My hand extended out, pretending to shake a man's hand.

Get the f-ing job, I whispered to myself.

Pregnancy concealed, determination high, I got the job.

Jeff and I, despite the recession happening around us, made it through the winter, grappling toward spring, when our restaurant would open its doors.

In March of 2009, it was time to hire Crêpe Cellar's opening team, so we took to the best online hiring tool available at the time: Craigslist. We posted jobs for hosts, servers, prep cooks, line cooks, sous chefs, kitchen managers, bartenders—the whole bit. We were starting from scratch.

With the recession crippling our city, more than two hundred people showed up to apply for jobs at our little eleven-table restaurant. A local TV station reported on the line out the door—not for meals, but for employment. Apparently, not many people were jumping into the restaurant business right then.

We hired a front-of-house team that was a little misfitty, untrained, and inexperienced, but it was our team. Mixed in with my dread and misgivings, I was surprised by a positive feeling I hadn't anticipated: the joy of creating opportunities for others. Quietly, I tucked that feeling into my heart—something special to hang on to. Of utmost importance, our first hire was our executive chef, Steve Kuney. He had been around various Charlotte restaurants that have since come and gone, including Lulu's, Cosmo's, and a fine dining spot in the Dilworth neighborhood called Bonterra. Steve worked with Jeff and Paul to develop the menu. Jeff wanted everything to be homemade in our Crêpe Cellar kitchen, and there was a lot to learn.

In many ways, we had a bumpy start entering the restaurant business. But it was still a start—and that proved enough to get momentum going in the direction of the dream.

From the get-go at Crêpe Cellar, per Jeff's request, we made all our food in-house from crêpes, sauces, rubs, and dressings, to our hand-cut, twice-fried french fries, purple slaw, and pesto for our brussels sprouts. We served reasonably priced half carafes of wine just like we had enjoyed in street cafés in France, Italy, and Spain. We aimed toward a cozy European gastropub—and we had nailed it, as best we could with the budget we had.

Looking around our tiny restaurant, you wouldn't have seen a custom-designed floor or decorative wallpaper to pull together design elements like we do now. You wouldn't have seen top-of-the-line glassware or super-expensive bottles of wine. You wouldn't have seen special equipment to offer hand towels at the end of dinner service, no Verre de Vin (for storing open bottles of wine), nor a Hoshizaki machine for super-carbonated sparkling water. There was nothing earth-shattering about the concept. Crêpe

Cellar was a warm, inviting place with brown floor tones, cozy candles, and kind-hearted service. It was a simple experience, but beautiful in its simplicity because there were no frills, just delicious homemade food in a dark, busy room.

Crêpe Cellar was clearly an independent eating place—there were just three rows of tables, with banquettes perpendicular against the windows, a row of separate tables down the center of the room, and then a long banquette with tables and chairs that could be pushed together to flexibly seat guests. I'm sure there were hundreds, thousands of ways we could have done a better job, but we made do. With a little bit of grace to find a way—not just the proven way—we found ourselves moving forward using the pieces we had.

Opening night was upon us. When our doors unlatched at 5 p.m., people gathered outside waiting to join us for dinner. We had done our work. We had started basic social media marketing, and we had let newspapers know about our opening, reaching out cold to *Charlotte Observer* staff writers we had no connection to. A big part was just word of mouth. We were the talk of the city for a brief moment, in no small part because, while so many other restaurants were closing, our team was running into the fire with little confidence from the world around us that we could succeed.

People came all night. A couple hours in, we were three deep at the bar. Blue hues from the dark sky mixed with streetlights. And people stood as dark shadows in front of those moody outdoor lights—mostly people we didn't know. They showed up and gave us a shot. I dropped back behind the partial wall near the bathrooms and let out a stifled squeal of bliss.

I didn't stay long that night at Crêpe Cellar. I was pregnant, my feet were swollen, and I had a job to show up for in the morning. It *was* exhilarating, though, the pride, the hope, the people—all the yeses. Jeff came home late opening night exhilarated too. After a full, busy first night, Jeff and Paul agreed: It was the hardest $1,500 they had ever worked for. Opening night surpassed our hopes. It was more fun, more full, more exuberant—despite all the changes we'd need to make. We weren't there yet, but we were headed in a direction of success.

With no excess budget, from there it was the scrappy, out-of-the-box kind of effort that propelled us forward.

GOING OFF-RECIPE

NoDa, the neighborhood where Crêpe Cellar was located, held Friday night gallery crawls for which people came from all over the city to immerse themselves in an eclectic experience that they could safely return home from and remember as an adventure. The streets were filled on gallery crawl nights, and art crawlers became our target market for our new restaurant.

Starting a few months before Crêpe Cellar opened, I had rolled out a hip-high old wooden beer barrel to the street and set a bar stool in the nook of our door. On top of the barrel, I placed a notebook and a pen. People walked by, and I'd smile and introduce them to the restaurant we were working on behind the boarded-up windows, collecting email addresses one at a time.

Then, I did it again the next week. And the next.

My notebook filled.

Before social media was rampant, we were grassroots marketing. No one email address was critical, but en masse, they were beneficial. When you start from nothing, there's value in the very small things, and we were wringing out value from whatever we could find.

We still, almost exclusively, use social media marketing methodologies over a dozen years later. For restaurants and many businesses, about 5 percent of revenue is invested back into the business as marketing dollars. We don't do that. We don't spend on magazine ads, radio, billboards, or other traditional resources. It's tempting to jump on advertising as a cure-all—and sometimes it can be effective—but throwing money at these outlets is not the same thing as effectively connecting with guests. Our organic social interactions primarily had a financial purpose at first (they saved us a lot of money!), but as the years passed, those authentic interactions proved to be remarkably valuable.

Our digital communication improved as we learned what people wanted to see and how they wanted to interact with us. We took the camera behind the scenes to show research and development for new dishes, the process of our menu tastings, and how to make favorites like our homemade burrata. It was never focused on selling crêpes or burgers or carafes of wine. Softer marketing efforts take longer to be effective, but because we built connection and community, they proved to be more powerful and long-lasting.

To this day, we spend our marketing dollars on a salaried marketing team, so we have our own people telling our story. If we're telling an authentic story, people will react positively by sharing it with their friends, digitally or by word of mouth. It's a long-play strategy that requires patience as the story builds, but it has produced resilient results.

As Charlotte grew and more restaurants opened, being "us" became one of our biggest differentiation points in our story. Chefs come to open restaurants in Charlotte with James Beard awards and Michelin Stars—and highly acclaimed restaurant groups with a whole lot more advertising dollars bring followings from other cities—but no one else will ever be *us*. Pivoting toward the personal was key to our survival and remains essential to thriving over the long haul. It's a little "off-recipe," but you can see it clearly in our restaurant group's unusual, uncatchy name: Tonidandel-Brown Restaurant Group. It's not flashy, it's not *typical*; it's authentically us.

Perhaps Jeff and I adopted somewhat unexpected tactics just because we had never been in the restaurant business. We didn't know any better. We did things our way, a little "off-recipe," because we didn't have preconceived notions of how things should be. That "detriment" may have been one of our greatest superpowers.

For the first six years Crêpe Cellar was open, we didn't take reservations. Reservations were inefficient. We had plenty of walk-ins, and we filled seats fast enough. Tables didn't sit empty waiting for patrons with reservations to show up. It was fluid yet consistent with all walk-in guests. Over time, though, our guests wanted to celebrate special occasions with us—anniversaries, birthdays, or promotions. They'd have to rely on our walk-in system, and likely not get a table when they wanted.

Offering reservations made sense to provide better hospitality, but we had two main holdups. One, if we took reservations, tables could sit empty for lengthy times before a party showed up. This is especially common with large parties. If you push three tables together (a four-top and two two-tops), you have a table for eight guests. But if the group is dining at 7:30 p.m., you cannot seat any of those tables past 6 p.m. in case the earlier parties stay at the table past the expected ninety minutes. Now you have three tables sitting vacant for an hour. Then if the party is late, there's another fifteen minutes lost. Large parties tend to stay a long time, which can be great, but it means you're only getting one turn off those three tables. If you have a lot of walk-ins and no reservations, on the other hand, those tables are filled and turning perhaps three times over the night.

The second issue stems from the significant change in how diners treat reservations. Increasingly, diners are quick to dismiss their reservations and simply not show up. They don't call to cancel either. One Valentine's Day, a friend of ours in the business had no-shows at more than 80 percent of his reserved tables. This can happen any night of the week, but it's even more common on special occasion nights like New Year's Eve or Valentine's Day because people make reservations at multiple places and then neglect or forget to cancel.

Cancellations and low turnovers are sour lemons in our world, but we've found a different way of approaching them. Many professionals in the industry go straight to third-party systems for reservations. These systems typically have great results through Google or other search engines, so their links pop up higher in searches. They also have more language options for users and good name recognition, but they're costly for restaurants.

Third-party systems exist for their own benefit. If your restaurant doesn't have openings at the time the searcher is hoping for, third-party systems suggest other restaurant options that have openings at that time, as opposed to offering other days to come visit *your* restaurant. Many third-party reservation systems don't care whether the diner chooses to reserve at a specific place; they just want the diner to reserve a table *somewhere*. That's how they make money. You may very well lose potential guests to alternative suggestions made by your third-party system "partner."

In addition, restaurants currently pay third-party systems about $1 per person when a guest makes a reservation. Instead of paying a third-party system, there's value to harvest for your own restaurant, which is what we did at each of our sit-down spots.

Each day, guests can walk up to one of our restaurants that take reservations and ask for a table, and if there isn't a table, they can put themselves on a waitlist. If, however, a guest wishes to make a reservation in advance to *guarantee* a seat at one of our restaurants, they can do that through our system. We charge a nonrefundable $2 to $3 per seat for that guarantee, depending on the restaurant and the day of the week.

At Supperland, our "steakhouse meets church potluck" concept, where the math proves easiest as an example, the average guest spends about $100. In the average restaurant, with a per-guest check of $100 and an average profit margin between 3 and 5 percent, the take-home profit for the restaurant would be between $3 and $5 per diner. We average 10 percent profit, or $10 per guest. One of the ways we get to that figure is through our unique reservation system. When a guest purchases a reservation for $3, we are starting at a $3 profit before they even read the menu.

There certainly can be drawbacks to this system. You have to have a busy, steady restaurant that draws in a lot of guests, or you'll turn away potential patrons. Over the years, we have had comments and complaints about our nonrefundable reservation fee too. People don't want to be charged for a reservation, or they want the charge to go toward their bill. But we look at it differently. We've monetized the value of convenience and a guaranteed table. Knowing the inefficiencies reservations can cause throughout a shift, we would just as soon skip them altogether. But if people want to pay for the guarantee, they can—and if they have paid for it, they are likely to show up. As it turns out, a reservation is the most profitable item we sell. We saw a gap in demand and found a way to capitalize on it—not to be conniving but to give guests another option. Plus, we did it in a way that would expand our profit margins and bring more security to our business and the jobs we provide.

ONE OPPORTUNITY LEADS TO ANOTHER

When you're stepping forward, no matter the smoothness of the path, you're led to new things, new opportunities, new doors that crack open. For us, that all started with eleven tables at Crêpe Cellar, and within the first year, with all our tending, the small seeds we had planted began to sprout and grow.

As Crêpe Cellar's one-year anniversary came around, a new opportunity presented itself. It was 2010; bank jobs in Charlotte continued to get slashed, and restaurants and retail shops were closing on every corner, including the corner of Thirty-Fifth and North Davidson, right next door to Crêpe Cellar. With few other options, our landlord asked if we'd consider expanding our successful eleven-table restaurant into the space next door.

It was kind of a surprise that within a year, our success was clear enough that we were talking to our landlord about expanding, even if we didn't lean into the idea right away. Crêpe Cellar was successful in part because of its intimacy and charm, and we didn't want to ruin that by expanding the dining room too quickly. But we were willing to toy with the idea of opening a different concept altogether. There had been many industry cases showing that restaurants stacked side by side don't necessarily compete with one another; instead, they invigorate the dining scene for all.

We went for it, and as with Crêpe Cellar, Jeff teamed up with Paul to create the concept. My role was secondary, but I spearheaded the naming of the place, consulted generally on the design direction, and in the evenings, I helped Jeff work on the menu, developing panini sandwiches with different meats, cheeses, and sauces on our George Foreman grill, and hand-ground sausage stuffed in our apartment kitchen. It wasn't glamorous, but I weirdly loved learning how sausage was made, getting to help develop the menu, working with my hands, and observing Jeff and Paul's plans. I had one foot in, one foot out—knowing my enjoyment of making the place had to be tempered to realistically split time between our new baby, Isabella; my breadwinning job; and being the supportive wife of a new restaurateur.

Growlers Pourhouse opened in August of 2010, just a year and a half after Crêpe Cellar. The concept keyed in on Jeff's passion for craft beer. Jeff was Charlotte's first Certified Cicerone (like a sommelier of beer), and we centered our food menu to pair with a curated list of fourteen beers, all selected by style. With a meager kitchen at Growlers Pourhouse, we cut a hole in the back-of-house brick wall so it could capitalize on the equipment next door at Crêpe Cellar. Our two side-by-side restaurants would share a cooking space, both of them led by Chef Steve Kuney. As time passed, Growlers Pourhouse would make the list of the Top 100 Beer Bars in the Country by *Draft Magazine* five years in a row.

We suddenly had two restaurants and a team of about forty people working across both places to put out two very different menus. Despite the different end products, we relied a lot on cross-utilizing ingredients. The fries at Crêpe Cellar had homemade pesto and brie, while those same fries at Growlers Pourhouse were served with a beer cheese. We made homemade sausage links and bratwurst for the Growlers menu, but chopped down, that sausage could be used in pasta specials at Crêpe Cellar. The raw oysters we put on a tray with cocktail sauce at Growlers were fried up and tossed in a buffalo sauce at Crêpe Cellar to top an entrée salad.

The two concepts complemented each other well—and intentionally so. The small Growlers Pourhouse menu was centered around homemade sausage, which could conveniently be made in advance and warmed up when orders came in, putting less stress on the busy shared kitchen. Oysters could be shucked on the line with no cooking required. As Crêpe Cellar hit peak time at 7:30 p.m., Growlers was just receiving its first guests for the evening. Peak time at Growlers was closer to 10 p.m. and sometimes later, with nighttime crowds staying until 2 a.m. With a shared kitchen space and staff, managing the two together was a choreographed daily dance of logistics.

In hindsight only do I see that taking steps forward is what led to more possibilities. It was a bold first step to open Crêpe Cellar—but that bravery is what made steps two, three, four, and five possible.

MEET WALLS HEAD-ON

When you step in boldly, sometimes things come easily, and those new opportunities present themselves, like they did for our creation of Growlers Pourhouse. But other times they don't, and that doesn't mean you need to shrivel.

In 2012, Jeff and I, on one of our inspiration walks around the city, had our eyes out for a possible location for a newly brewing restaurant concept we had in mind. We hoped to find a spot in the historic Dilworth neighborhood of Charlotte, where we had just bought our first house to settle in with our growing family, welcoming our little boy, Eli, into our fold. We were now parents of two.

Charlotte had become home, and we rooted our family in a 1904 fixer-upper that, even a dozen years later, never quite got the fixing up it needed. The windows had rope pulls, and on windy Carolina nights, I'd stuff a sock or a washcloth in the panes to keep them from rattling. One stormy night, water poured from our bathroom upstairs, through the dining room fixtures, and all over our table and floor. We poured buckets out of those fixtures the next morning. Slanted floors led around every room, and some even had one-inch step-ups that we had grown accustomed to stepping over, but guests would catch their feet on the unexpectedly uneven ground. The house, as a dollhouse Victorian, was one of the original spec homes of the Latta Park community within the larger Dilworth neighborhood.

As many imperfections as our house had, it also had incredible charm. Pink stained glass intersected in the corner of our bathroom, and an awkward primary-color stained glass window hung on the other side of the same room. Gorgeous thick fireplaces graced nearly every room, though most of the chimneys had been bricked or boarded over by the time we bought the house. The stairs creaked, the stair railing swayed outward, the ceilings had cracks of time, and the walls waved in and out. But it was home.

Our neighborhood of Dilworth had all the beautiful historic touches too. The community had been Charlotte's first suburb, starting with the advent of a streetcar that rolled from downtown out to Latta Park (located in Dilworth and not far from Atherton Mills, where the textile industry boomed in the early part of the twentieth century). As one of many stately former residences that dotted East Boulevard on a main strip in Dilworth, there it was—an available building that had been recently serving as a commercial office. The former house seemed perfect for a new restaurant concept we were formulating, Haberdash House, which would be a nod to the neighborhood's textile mill history. We envisioned a charming two-story dining room and southern dishes. It had a small parking lot nestled in the back and an area for a lovely bricked-in patio. You could quickly see how a table in the front window, set beautifully with candles and calm lighting, would entice people driving by. There would be tricks to working a multistory restaurant, but we were up for the challenge.

To put our concept in that former house, we'd need to get the property rezoned for a restaurant tenant. Jeff and I had never rezoned a property before, but it didn't take us long to realize how difficult that endeavor was going to be.

As with any rezone, the neighbors held a community meeting to give feedback and share concerns. We walked into the room, an upstairs hall of sorts in an old church building, filled with folding chairs. The lighting was spotty and unwelcoming, the air cool and damp.

I sat with our two toddlers against the back wall as several people entered the room. It was a small group, and everyone sat in chairs apart from one another. If they knew each other, it wasn't well enough to share a row. After a few minutes, Jeff, our attorney, and our architect walked to the front of the room. They pulled up a PowerPoint to present our plan for Haberdash House, seated on busy East Boulevard, across from a strip mall that included a Harris Teeter supermarket, a Lebanese restaurant, and a Smoothie King. Our proposed project would require the rezoning of this former house, located next to a gas station but butting up against a neighborhood of single-family homes. Our team made it through three slides before the questions started firing. Apparently, minds had been made up on the project prior to the meeting, and this group didn't approve.

Loud attendees, who couldn't speak without standing and leaning forward, pelted questions at our fumbling team. Broad, harsh gestures flooded toward the front of the room. Helpless, I doled out crayons and stickers to the children as they colored trees in a palette of rainbows, wondering how to look at these neighborly faces in the same light again. We weren't positioned to defend our case without escalating the situation.

In the aftermath of that meeting, protestors created a Facebook page against the project. The page clamored about our existing restaurants and bemoaned the evils of bringing a restaurant into that East Boulevard space. Not enough parking. Too much noise. A dumpster, with dumpster sounds. Debauchery and drunkenness into all hours of the night.

We'd hoped and planned to do something invigorating for our new neighborhood, but our efforts invoked fear of change, anger, and attack. After about a week, as the brash negativity roared onward, we walked away from the space.

Maybe we gave up too easily; we were young and new at development projects. No longer sweet and exciting, the project rotted like a maggot-filled piece of meat. Between attorney and architectural fees, we lost $20,000—a big hit for a young couple—not to mention the thwarted dream to put a restaurant in our own neighborhood. I took the loss very personally, too personally. Jeff and I agreed: Never again would we try to open a restaurant in Dilworth.

This loss hurt a lot, and because of the personal nature, it was hard to dig out and get back up. But looking back, that failure and the lessons learned were nothing more than guideposts to get us to a better position. It's just sometimes hard to see that in the moment.

Haberdash House was an ill-fated concept that fell victim to a failed rezone, but with our world rooting itself in both Charlotte and in food and drink, we couldn't let the idea go. Even without a physical home yet, Haberdash House had legs. There was something luring us to grow our idea and explore the city's culinary roots and history of food.

Charlotte originated as a Native American trading post. The city isn't located on water, which is unusual for a city of our size. We have influences from all over the South, but specifically from the Appalachian Mountains, from which many people flocked to cities for mill jobs in the early twentieth century. There are also heavy influences from the North Carolina Piedmont—the area between the coast and the Appalachian Mountains—where farms focused on corn, wheat, chicken, and pork. Charlotte had some unique cuisine influences from the rivers that pass on the outskirts, too, where fish camps served up small fish and crawfish sautéed, stewed, or fried. Traditional dishes from these areas continue to play a role in what is considered North Carolinian cuisine, or even more specifically, Charlotte cuisine.

Our bold dream was to weave these influences together in a new restaurant that might play a part in defining Charlotte's food heritage. As we visited restaurants all over the Southeast, we began to home in on a simple starting point: fried chicken. With fried chicken as the centerpiece of our burgeoning concept, we would develop thoughtful, hearty southern sides and homemade desserts to go alongside. The menu items would represent the heart and soul of Charlotte's traditional food history and serve to share stories about the area that had become our home. It was an area with a diverse range of influences, brought centrally together in the Queen City with the rise of the industrial textile mills that popped up in the early 1900s, drawing in migrants from all over the Carolinas.

A year passed until we found another possible location for our dreamed-up fried chicken concept, and to our surprise, it had been sitting in plain view all along. It was in NoDa, just a couple doors down from Crêpe Cellar.

The day we signed the lease on this new NoDa project was the day I gave my notice at my salaried job. The dream Jeff and I had imagined in Tarifa, Spain, and carried separately for years—was suddenly ours to build together.

Like Dilworth, NoDa was an area of the city that once bustled with textile mills, so our restaurant idea would still pay tribute to Charlotte's mill town history—just now we'd be opening two miles northeast of the center city. We mashed our original haberdashery-related name, Haberdash

House, with the word *dish* to form our new spot's name: Haberdish. Haberdish would open in the erstwhile general store of the former mill town of North Charlotte, familiarly known as NoDa.

Our research team consisted of Jeff, me, and now three children (Isabella and Eli had welcomed their new baby brother, Isaac, in February 2015), and we traveled from Charlotte to Asheville to Greenville to Atlanta, stopping off at the little towns in between. We scoured the region for ideas, ingredients, techniques, and touches we could incorporate into our menu. Sometimes it was a specific dish, like the North Carolina–born sonker, a delicious fruit dessert melding the ideas of cobbler and pie and often served with a creamy milk dip poured over. Other times it was ingredients, like bacon jam. We also collected touches to bolster our notion of a great cocktail program, with all syrups, garnishes, tonics, and ice made in-house.

Haberdish opened as a "southern mill town kitchen" with fried chicken and beautiful apothecary-style cocktails. This was our third restaurant on the same block, and it was crazy abuzz from the day it opened, bringing our team regional acclaim. We showed up in *Southern Living*'s Best Bars; the city selected us to represent Charlotte in *Our State Magazine*; our mixologist, Colleen Hughes, was featured in *USA Today* and *Popular Mechanics*. People weren't just visiting us from the neighborhood or even from the city. Our guests were coming from other cities—and other regions—to taste this unique, fun take on southern food.

Acclaim is great, but it was what Haberdish did for us as a couple that was most pivotal for me and Jeff. We'd been in the restaurant business for six years, but it was Haberdish that finally made our dream of being in the family restaurant business *together* a reality. We didn't know it at the time, but we were at a turning point.

SERVING SPOON: Look closely at where you are and where you want to go. Sometimes it just takes one bold step toward it for the process to begin unfolding.

Three

CREATE WITH INTENTION

Write your own life recipe.

B eing new to any business opens opportunities to beautiful, savory bites on the path to success. Freedom from prior experience allows for spontaneous sprinklings of nutmeg, spritzes of lime, or edible flower garnishes not in the original recipe. Jeff and I didn't plan for certain ingredients to play such big roles in our growth, but those extra sprinkles, spritzes, and garnishes have played a huge part in serving up success. They were the creative elements, put in place with intention and passion and drive toward the making of something great.

LEAN ON PASSION

Creating with intention means creating what you actually dream of—what's stirring in your heart. That passion means the idea remains with you in good times and bad. That passion carries through when there's progress, and when there's none at all. It pushes the creation forward because you want it so badly and you believe in it so much that you're willing to work through the muck to get to the other side and see your creation come to life.

We first walked into the mid-century church in Plaza Midwood three years before our restaurant Supperland would come to life there. We went just to see the building, just to see "what if"? On that initial visit, Jeff had been given the key to the padlock on the plywood door. He fidgeted with it before swinging the door open to a massive room with rafters exposed above and rough suede-like walls with black-and-white patches melded to grays and cream colors rising from the floor to the raftered ceiling. Windows, five on each side, escalated up the walls with light pouring through the oaks outside onto the ground. A two-toned floor where carpet had been lifted traced the aisle that had once separated the two sides of church pews. On the back side of the room, a walled-in structure a couple feet off the ground held pieces of the former baptismal spigot, which had been covered over for years while the building served as a gallery, bead shop, and art shop. With two buildings, two stories, and a raw, unfinished basement, the place could be turned into anything.

Located about one mile east of the center city, the building had been a church with two separate buildings on a triangular corner lot. The smaller building was the original sanctuary built in 1948; the larger structure was built in 1956 once the congregation had saved enough money to expand to a larger footprint. The building needed structural work. It needed to be rezoned in order to become a restaurant. Plus, there were issues with parking.

But while we were distracted with other potential projects, eventually (about a year and a half later) the rezone slid quietly through with the landlord's leadership, and the property could suddenly be used as a restaurant. The landlord also finished the necessary structural requirements and resolved the parking issues. Suddenly it was a very viable project for us.

A list of hand-scratched words in my messy, pencil-sketch-studded notebook showed the name *Supperland* with a large circle around it, and a star—like maybe that could be the name for our next concept, a quirky Southern "steakhouse meets church potluck."

We tackled that behemoth of a project, Supperland, with a staggering challenge we never could have foreseen—a worldwide pandemic.

There were days we made zero progress—but it was hard to make that the priority. This was when many people were afraid to leave their houses. I was gloved, wiping down my groceries with antibacterial wipes on my porch before bringing them inside to put them away. We weren't visiting people at their houses. Even as warmer weather came in early spring, I only permitted our kids to play with one other family's kids—and it had to be outside. Our "bubble" was tight.

No one was dining out. Our business had been chipped away to nothing, and we had no idea what was coming next, how the rules were changing, or how we'd ever get out of the financial hole. There were a lot of things to think about beyond the massive project we had initiated in that old church.

In Charlotte, construction was permitted to continue, but getting workers to show up at a job site was another story. They were encouraged to stay home at the slightest sign of sickness. Then there were the compounding supply issues, which brought progress to a halt many times.

We had taken the smaller building on the property, which we envisioned as a bar, down to studs, and it sat untouched for months. Sometimes I wanted to be near the building even if there was nothing I could do, like if I just gave it attention by showing up, maybe that would help it move forward.

One day in the middle of the week, with school closed and nothing (again) on the schedule, our three kids—now eleven, eight, and five years old—and I packed up a plastic bag of small paint containers. There were the standard yellow hues from lemon to marigold, and reds from mauve to rose. But we also had the real winners like hot pink with silver glitter, and creamy white with blue confetti. We stuffed in a handful of paintbrushes, paper towels, and paper cups. Our project: Paint the studs of the bar.

Over the course of a week, the kids and I brought our paints and brushes and covered the studs with our artwork. Bold color blocks in a rainbow stretched across black-and-white striped patterns. A large vase extended upward with white leaflets hanging from thin stems. A rainbow, painted sideways and bookended by white fluffy clouds, sat underneath a baby chick, coming into the picture as Easter approached. Brushstrokes of a five-year-old swiped lines that resembled small trees, a red bird, and a solid blue stripe of sky with a marker-drawn sun and clouds in gold and white.

Months later, these creations were covered over; eventually, much more refined floral wallpaper concealed our work. But in that time, our family painting sessions brought an unearthly, innocent positive energy toward the project we loved—despite no tangible progress being made. I guess it was passion without progress.

We continued building even as people were predicting that restaurants would become a thing of the past, even when some suggested that no one would visit large restaurants anymore, ever. The industry, many feared, would change so significantly that most would go out of business.

We kept building. We were driven to bring our grand dining hall to life, and despite the naysaying, we pressed on with the belief that someday people would come through our doors and be overjoyed with what we had created in the shallows of a pandemic.

By default, menu creation for Supperland was radically different from anything we had ever done. A lot of the early development happened on the back deck of our house, with between five and seven chefs cooking over our backyard grills or bringing potluck dishes to share and discuss. Everything we did was outside in the fresh air, no full kitchen, no proper equipment. We made do.

A slow building process is often frustrating, and this one was, but in time, the delays set us up for an ideal opening time. By the end of 2020, much of our equipment—including our fourteen-foot custom grill and wood-fired oven—was in place. As the space began to take shape, Jeff, the kids, our executive chef, Chris Rogienski—who we brought over from Haberdish—and I met in the evenings at the restaurant. We practiced cooking over our new wood-fired grill to further our menu development. From the beginning, we had a broad leaning toward a steakhouse, but with our vision of "church potluck" influences, we were charting new territory.

As the process continued, our team grew. We hired a general manager, Jon Rosenberg, who joined us in our evening cooking rituals. We invited small friend groups so we could practice dishes. Our practice nights grew to twenty people—everyone spaced out throughout the room, masked up. Jeff and Chef Chris tended the fire cooking, and Jon and I worked the front of the house, delivering dishes to tables and bussing.

We had a huge restaurant to lift off the ground, but with the constraints of COVID, we had to do it in pieces and parts. We interviewed, hired, and trained our staff and opened in March 2021. There were still plenty of COVID restrictions in place. We could only have 50 percent capacity. There was a citywide curfew at 10 p.m. We had to respect six-foot spacing. Our team was required to be masked.

There were so many reasons to stop along the way, but we poured ourselves into Supperland however we could. We had a vision, and while all normal courses toward opening were closed off to us, there was a way. We loved that place from the start, and that passion eventually showed through when our doors opened and we welcomed droves of guests in to experience our creation for the first time.

RAISE EXPECTATIONS

We weren't always great at having high expectations; sometimes on our journey we thought too small. If I could give my younger self some advice, I'd surely say, "Think bigger; raise your expectations." Smaller thinking will bring smaller outcomes. The opposite is also true.

When we opened Supperland, we had three red meat cuts on the menu, all of which we cooked on the wood-fired grill: filet, ribeye, and flanken. The filet and ribeye were cooked to medium-rare on the fire with salt, pepper, and a heavy brush of beef tallow. The flanken was our cheaper cut, served as three slabs topped with a tightly chopped horseradish gremolata with parsley, lemon zest, and garlic.

However, we learned quickly, as flanken sales declined over the first year, that people were choosing the better cuts of meat. When any item on a menu is lagging in sales, first we theorize why, and then we figure out whether we need a replacement. When flanken sales dropped, we had options: offer only two steak cuts, switch to a different cheaper cut, or find something that elevated the menu, pushing guests beyond our prime filet and prime ribeye to an even more premium cut.

One Tuesday afternoon at Supperland, about seven of us sat around a long table, ready to taste a sample of a premium steak cut: Australian Wagyu New York strip with a marbling score of eight; a high-end—and expensive—cut. Chef Chris flipped the steak over the fire, sprinkled the salt and pepper, and gave it a brisk swipe of tallow. The strip steak rested, then was sliced into thin pieces shingled across the plate. The first fork-fuls hit our mouths: buttery and salty, hints of fire and smoke, rich, soft, and a little funky too. I had never tasted anything like it. Heads nodded around the table, and our discussion shifted to whether our guests would pay $120 for a 16-ounce cut, which is what we would need to charge to meet our food costs. Ultimately, we wanted to give our guests the best food experiences available, and the Wagyu strip went on the menu. That same night, we sold six Wagyu steaks—more than we'd expected for the price point—and our sales on the item only grew.

High expectations make a big difference on a single menu item, but some-times an elevated aspiration has a much grander effect. When Supperland opened in 2021, the place was special—the decor touches, the unusual menu, the food, the custom plates, the awe of stepping in the door. But those wonders were only accessible to those who came in person. Jeff and I wanted to share the special place we'd built with people beyond our city. Could the regional acclaim we'd earned with Haberdish, which had opened in 2016, help raise our visibility with well-known food writers across the country?

I feared the former acclaim wouldn't be enough. The distance between where we were as a local restaurant group and where I imagined we could be in the national restaurant scene seemed vast, like a task only a big public relations agency (with an agency-sized budget) could effectively tackle. How could we make the right connections to get Supperland in front of the biggest, loudest foodie voices?

Though I had my doubts, I scoured websites and Instagram to compile a list of writers and editors to contact. The people on my list were so much bigger than me, they were so much more well-known and well-respected in the food world. Why would they ever write me back, and why would they care about this beautiful but quirky restaurant in Charlotte? I set the list aside and closed my eyes. All the *I wishes* fluttered around. I had to find a way for us to be seen.

Vision boards can be powerful strategy tools. I pulled photos from the internet and some from my camera: colorful, inviting foods, family photos, and lovely interiors of commercial spaces that I'd want to visit. Then I included two things about Supperland: a photo of the front covers of four *Bon Appétit* magazines fanned out and a photo of a rigged-up magazine spread I had made with computer paper doctored up with handwritten words and titles as if *Bon Appétit* had actually written an article about us. Those two images sat beside each other in the top right corner of my vision board.

While I had been toying around with the notion, the magic of Supperland's first night made one thing very clear: We *needed* to think bigger. The chandeliers glistened with light passing through orb-like bulbs, welcoming and warm. The guests marveled upon entrance, heads turning up to gaze around the wide space. People were awed by the smoky teapots carrying ember butter to the table for roasted oysters, the lift of a pot roast lid, the bubbling of the onions, the flames dramatically rising from the open kitchen. It was different. The grand dining hall had come to life, now decorated with fancy, dressed-up people, ready for the occasion and ready to eat. The first night was living proof that Supperland was special. So I got brave.

My fingers pecked out an Instagram message to the new editor of *Bon Appétit*, Dawn Davis. She didn't yet have the gigantic following a lot of the magazine's other staff members had. Maybe she'd read my note. That very day, she responded and wished us well with the early weeks of the opening. All I could think was: *She wrote me back.*

Throughout 2021 and into 2022, I sent her short notes, keeping her posted on Supperland's articles and mentions. I let her know we'd flipped our first concept, Crêpe Cellar, into the new Ever Andalo. A year passed since my first reach out to her, but in May 2022, we received an email from Meryl Rothstein at *Bon Appétit*. The magazine wanted to include Supperland in an upcoming issue. Though we were all stunned, we coordinated a few things and held a couple of video calls too—everything to get the magazine what they needed. We had never had national attention like this before and didn't know what to expect.

One month later, as I worked from home, comfy on my couch, I got a call from Jeff. "Check your email," he said.

Elazar Sontag, the restaurant editor at *Bon Appétit*, sat at the top of my inbox: "By now you've already heard from an editor at BA about contributing recipes or being interviewed for an upcoming print issue. I wanted to be the first to tell you that the issue you'll be featured in is our October restaurant issue, because we're naming your restaurant one of America's 10 Best New Restaurants."

I slumped to the floor and sobbed.

No words, just heaves of air and tears all mixed into an uncontrollable outburst. *America's 10 Best New Restaurants?* We weren't on anyone's radar. We were in Charlotte, the little neighborhood of Plaza Midwood, on our triangular corner, with an unusual concept and an unknown team. It took me thirty minutes to get off the floor, partly from gratitude, partly from humility, partly from not wanting the moment of bliss to pass.

The *Bon Appétit* restaurant issue hit stands that October. From that moment, our sales jumped 40 percent. Our team rose to the occasion, and the energy only heightened. No longer did we want to belong with the best; we were among the best. And every bit of what we did and what we expected of ourselves continued to rise. Being named one of America's 10 Best New Restaurants didn't just bring us more business. It catapulted our whole restaurant group to a different level of thinking.

TELL A STORY

A restaurant is a living, breathing piece of art. People walk inside and become part of the shared experience for a moment of their lives. Not a single other type of business gets the opportunity to evoke so many different senses for their guests. Since people are moved by different things, by increasing the number of thoughtful ways we interact with guests, we intentionally connect with nearly every person who walks through our doors. Like a layered lasagna, Jeff and I build in dozens of intentional touch points, or elements, for our guests to interact with to provide memorable and lasting sensory experiences, made all the more delicious because of the blended components. After all, a bite of that lasagna is only complete when you dig down, top to bottom, and get every layer on your fork. As Jeff and I have grown and gotten better at what we do, the layers of our storytelling get richer and deeper.

The space or location can bring meaning to a restaurant, acting as an element connecting the guest to the brand. We're drawn to older buildings because they make the space itself a rich element to lean into—uncovering stories from the structure's past. In a newer space, there might be history from the street, the neighborhood, a prior owner, or even gleaned from the city's stories or myths. In a newer space, you could also lean into personal family stories or recipes or experiences an owner may have had. Some brands slide nicely into new spaces with a story built around a mission to support a cause.

In our newest restaurant concept, Leluia Hall, Jeff and I were very intentional in blending detailed layers, unique touches, and intriguing moments throughout the dining experience. That's because across many areas of life, people are craving *experiences*. Guests are greeted at the front door in a lounge area. A raw bar busily slices sushi-grade fish and plates up seafood towers that "smoke" as they pass through the dining room, with dry ice pellets creating a dramatic effect. Shareable family style dining allows guests to converse over dipping sauces and pour-overs and finger foods, before diving into shareable main entrées like our sugar steaks, saffron honey chicken, or lobster Thermidor with roasted root vegetables and lump crab.

We've equipped each guest with "eating tongs"—small, easy-to-use tongs that help guests elegantly pull raw fish from a seafood tower and dip it into sauces. The "eating tongs" are memorable and unique, but incredibly utilitarian as well. The bar puts out slushy cocktails with bold garnishes and warming cocktails with notes of spices, all of which invite our guests to stay a while. A wine list of over two hundred bottles escalates the experience.

The Leluia Hall space is a gigantic part of the story, too, because of the continued public interest in adaptive reuse projects. Leluia Hall brings modernity to a historical space. As Charlotte and the whole country continue toward growth, more advanced technology, and denser populations, old spaces increase in value. Our 1915 church building is more highly esteemed by being what it is. There's inherent value in a restaurant with character and charm—people love to bring friends and family to a unique restaurant with interesting architecture. It's the wide, rugged beams that hang overhead, the hundred-year-old slate and bricks that cover the building, the stories inside the room, the arching windows that look outdoors to trees sixty feet high.

As we shared our buildout story of this adaptive reuse project on social media, we built a following of supporters. We brought followers along through our first construction project when Jeff, Bryce Plott, and Jason Laughlin (our two construction mavens) confined themselves to the attic to connect long structural supports into the cracked beams to carry the weight of the roof. They came along when the kitchen's drywall was removed to uncover floating metal wall joists that had rusted and rotted two inches off the ground. We shared when we successfully removed the original prayer rail from the mezzanine level and donated it to the congregation that first built the church structure. Our followers, many of whom would someday be guests, joined us through the celebrations and challenges of building out the restaurant from scratch.

Besides utilizing the space itself, market research has always played an indelible role in our intentional planning and brand story. We work to understand the business climate so we can create concepts with lasting power. Each business plan we've written includes up-to-date statistics and food trends in support of our ideas to entice investors to our vision. When we were new at this business, we didn't look much past restaurant and dining trends. As the industry has shifted, however, restaurants aren't merely about the food, so we consider broader trends as well, even across different industries.

For example, as we worked on the Leluia Hall concept, we found people continued to gravitate their spending toward experiential dining, not just belly-stuffing menus; national chains were less enticing than independent restaurants; seafood was a big trend in restaurants, both for the health benefits and for the daunting nature of seafood preparation at home; and dietary individualism—for taste preferences and aversions as well as allergies and sensitivities—had become the norm.

Beyond food trends, cultural shifts play into our concepts in creative, thoughtful, brand-building ways. After being cooped up for much of 2020, the next couple of years brought in an escapism movement. People longed for leisurely escapes to anywhere but home, and that inspired design shifts that welcomed nature indoors, with bright tropical colors and patterns throughout a room; textures like rattan, cane, and wicker; and for us, inspired, colorful menus filled with fresh seafood and bright citrus flavors. When you visit one of Jeff's and my restaurants, we want you to step out of ordinary life in Charlotte and step into a reprieve from the norm, a two-hour escape to joy and delight. Leluia Hall leans strongly into this escapism trend.

Jeff and I don't always have specific statistics backing up the macro trends we discover; sometimes we rely on a gut feel. We live restaurant life every day. Fads rise and fall. Neighborhoods shift with growth. What sells sometimes changes. An awareness of how our city is growing, what it needs, and what is working (and not working) is sometimes impossible to measure.

Personal interests drive our inspiration too. But we pay attention to broader trends and put them in context with what we see locally, which gives us a solid foundation from which to create. In the end, all these elements—from the space to the market trends to a gut feel—are the roots of telling a story, which builds that dining experience, which delights our guests, which enchants them to return one visit after another.

GIVE THEM MORE

The product itself (the food) is a huge element of the brand story for our restaurants—sometimes outright, sometimes more subtly. But even food is never just food; there's opportunity to elevate menu items with educational elements, experiences, memorability, and uniqueness.

One of my favorite examples in our world is the olive oil flight at Ever Andalo—our Italian spot that replaced Crêpe Cellar after COVID. Our homemade focaccia is served with a three-bay olive oil flight, delivered with a card describing each of the oils, their flavor notes, and where they come from. The guest virtually travels to different regions of Italy, experiencing unique tastes, color variations, and aromas of olive oil. If we served olive oil on a plate, no one would complain, but the olive oil flight builds our story and connects the guest to our concept in a tangible way. The guest is experiencing. The guest is learning—specifically about Italian olive oils. The guest is participating in tasting much more than if we offered a cheap blended oil from the foodservice distributor. On a deeper level, the experience gives a greater appreciation for the nuances of olive oil and the notion that our restaurant goes to the trouble to bring in specific *Denominazione d'Origine Protetta* (DOP) olive oils from Italy. There is a sense of play as the guest tastes and learns favorites.

Likewise, the fresh-grated cheese at Ever Andalo couldn't just be *cheese*. We named the big pile of freshly grated Pecorino Romano or Parmigiano Reggiano—something you might get in a small ramekin for free at another establishment—a "cheese cloud," and we serve it on a plate piled high. Our cheese cloud has been featured in a local magazine, and its addition to any meal cannot be understated. Guests add it to the olive oil, top pastas with it, and even pile it on our vegetable side dishes.

Our absinthe service at the Bar at Supperland takes a similar approach. Many people have never tried absinthe, and certainly not from an ornate absinthe dispenser. The metal dispenser looks a little like a hookah—without the tubes and smoke—and it sits high on the table. Ours are silver and quite dramatic.

In the main liquid vessel is a high pour of water, which drips out of the dispenser from arms that jut out from the sides. We bring the dispenser to the table with all the arm valves closed, and the bartender places a glass under each arm. Every glass has a shot of absinthe at the bottom and a strainer spanning the glass to hold a sugar cube. The water from the dispenser drips onto the sugar cube and into the liquor beneath. Guests can water down the absinthe to their preference.

The drink is delicious, but the process itself is a conversation piece. It's an experience guests can't get everywhere, a moment to learn something new. They've tried absinthe in a traditional manner, and the offering helps set our bar and cocktail program apart. Whether or not the guest actually likes the drink (and we hope they do), it's still a gain for them because they've added an arrow to their foodie quiver.

To date, one of the most unique dining experiences we offer across our establishments is a recurring and rotating four-course meal in our Supperland speakeasy. What's so unusual is that our team creates these ten-week experiences by starting with our cocktail development. Usually, pairing menus begin in the kitchen with the food. For our speakeasy, however, our bartenders create incredibly innovative cocktails to fit a certain seasonal theme, and then our chefs get the challenge of pairing food to those drinks. There are only a handful of places in the world that take this cocktail-centric focus for a tasting menu.

The speakeasy space itself started out as an unfinished basement with an uneven Carolina red dirt floor. But being that it was tucked under our bar building, there seemed to be a way to use it for something special, something we couldn't easily execute in a larger space. When looking at it from a slightly different angle, there were wins with its tiny size. Carving out a walk-in and small prep area off to the side, we were left with a room that could showcase a small set of bar stools and a couple of tables. By fire code, we could only fit ten guests down there at a time, but our goal wasn't just to have a little bar area; we wanted to push the limits on what our bartenders could do with drink creation and execution.

The physical restraints proved to work in our favor, allowing us to give guests an incredibly unique experience. The room's intimacy allows our bartenders to do extraordinary cocktails. See, when our team is in the middle of a regular service at a full-scale bar, there are only so many touches we can put on a cocktail, only so much time to finish the drink and serve it. We're limited.

But with just ten people in a room, our bartenders create drinks with multiple steps and complicated processes. They've done drinks with fire over a cauldron-like bowl. They clarify a complex cocktail into a clear liquid with an hour-long centrifuge process. Some cocktails are mixed with up to seven different liquors. We've used handcrafted origami-like garnishes. The team uses liquid nitrogen to freeze and muddle mint leaves into a powder to top drinks.

The speakeasy was just a closed-in, ugly basement down a narrow set of stairs, but we made it a destination for a cocktail experience you can't replicate.

Memorable food experiences can also be simple. A savory, delightfully bitter olive oil pour-over accompanies our chocolate sorbet at Ever Andalo. Supperland serves a roasted oyster dish with a teapot of butter, smoking powerfully from an ember off our fire. The Supperland pot roast is served in a three-legged cast iron pot, and when the lid lifts, steam gusts upward, and guests ooh and aah. In the end, the goal with these dishes and the stories we create around them is to pull guests into the moment and guide them toward a richer time within our doors. Guests walk away with more than a full belly. They're enriched with food memories, potentially for the rest of their lives.

We all get stuck thinking like everyone else and following a path simply because it's already been paved. It's easier because someone else has done it, and you don't have to ask questions because it's already been proven to work. But what has served Jeff and me very well is bypassing assumptions about how things have been done in the past, and instead, adding a little thoughtfulness and creativity to come up with new ideas that can put forth something different, something more for our guests.

HAVE IT YOUR WAY

Every one of us is a unique expression of humanity. That means we each have a different perspective and a different way of doing things. By allowing your own way of doing things to shine through in your work, you're breaking norms and you're likely going to end up creating something unconventional—a product, business, process, or organization—and something that's far superior because you set things up the way *you* wanted to do it.

Naming our restaurant concepts is authentically unconventional. I start by making a mess on a lined sheet of paper, rows and rows of words applicable to our concept. Those rows turn into pages, and I circle words that have strong appeal or resonance to me. I pull in a thesaurus to expand the list of words. Sometimes I hop on Wikipedia or, more recently, Chat GPT to research topics and generate still more words. Then I begin playing with two or three words together to see how they fit, teasing out new combinations that could express our idea. When I came up with the name *Haberdish*, I was working on a project for my primary job, and the word *fish* was written on my paper. I also had the word *haberdashery* written at the bottom of the page. Somehow dots connected the sounds, and in pencil, I wrote down the word *Haberdish*.

Distinct, thoughtful names tee a business up for success. It takes courage to run with names that might need a little explaining and people may not get at first. Eventually, they'll understand, and the unique name will stick in people's minds.

For us, running our business has been about looking at restaurant processes in new ways and not accepting the norm as the rule. At Supperland, we've combined family style dining with fine dining. We've created a southern steakhouse with church potluck influences and still have hundreds of bottles on our wine list, hand-selected by a level-three sommelier. We have orchestrated silverware switch-outs throughout the meal and hot towels at the end of service. We offer caviar and whole lobster on the menu. On the other side, we have handcrafted tables with no tablecloths, unfinished patches on our walls, servers in golden aprons, homestyle Southern delicacies like ambrosia on the menu, and printed T-shirts for our food runners and server assistants. We deliberately clashed with traditional notions of "fine dining" to create something both fine and fun.

Still, one of the most unusual business practices we maintain is keeping many responsibilities in-house—including tasks that most restaurants outsource. There are so many components of running a restaurant that, for ease and expertise, it's sensible to outsource a lot of them: HVAC and equipment repair, pest control, landscaping, waste management, architecture, and engineering; the list is long. Partners ebb in and out of our operations every week, which is how 90 percent of our revenue sneaks back out the door. But there are some typically outsourced tasks we find *so* important that we do them ourselves.

Interior design is a job usually left to the pros, but Jeff and I bounce ideas off each other to collaborate on the interior plans at all our restaurants. Both of us are untrained, but we draw on our real-life experience and our vision. We count on each other to shoot down impractical ideas, bring new thoughts to a space, and curate interesting elements. We do this together because we never want a space to feel too "designed," too corporate, or too much like other spaces. For us, "good design" is pulling in a lot of different influences that play well together but in a unique way that builds the brand and shapes the experience of the restaurant. The result is aligned and authentic because no one knows the brand like we do.

We also design our own spaces together because we love that part. We don't want to pass off one of our favorite pieces—creating life in a new space—to someone else. The interior design of a restaurant is critical to the eventual restaurant experience. And for us, it works best when it originates in our minds.

Besides interior design, another huge part of a restaurant's buildout is millwork, and we keep that in-house too. Millwork covers elements like molding and custom cabinetry behind bars or in kitchens. When we've built out our larger spaces, the quotes for millwork have averaged over $100,000. We obviously save a lot of money because Jeff has the skills and equipment to do this work himself, along with the two guys on our team dedicated to woodshop work, handyman efforts, and building upkeep. This also gives us greater freedom to design. We draw up exactly what we want, Jeff models it out on his computer, and our team cuts it down by hand or with our computer numerical control machine (CNC), a computer-controlled router that cuts out wood in predesigned shapes.

For our tables, typically, I'll sketch the designs, mixing in solid tops with inlays or patterns depending on where they will be in the dining room. We go back and forth to refine the design and select types of wood to manifest our vision. Our woodworkers put together mockups of the tabletops. Once we're happy with the look, our team builds them to spec. This handmade process gives us not only unique tables but new layers of our story to share with guests. But we get even more granular than this.

I deliberated for over six months on what kind of flower vase to have at our concept Leluia Hall. There were plenty of options out there, but nothing was exciting to me. I'd set the project down and try again months later in the hopes that some company would release an intriguing piece. Then one day I saw a photo online of dried flowers sticking out of a smooth-edged wooden square block. The dots connected. I drew up a 3D image of an arched block with a simple V-shape design on the sides. The arch would mimic the shape of our windows, and the V shape subtly replicated a wheat pattern in our wallpaper. Jeff got on his computer and modeled it, then took it to the woodshop for the CNC machine to create them. They're darling and a one-of-a-kind, handmade item for our dining room.

Perhaps most importantly, we keep brand concept creation in-house. We lean on a graphic designer to develop a logo, but the story, the feel of the brand, the overall menu, and the full integration of the experience— including service points, order of operations, and the showmanship of different dishes—all this comes from our cohesive vision. This is a big piece in the art of making a restaurant, and it's where Jeff and I have the most potential impact on the success of a concept. We hold it close because it is where our touch is most significant.

The feel of our restaurants—from interior design to concept development and creating bespoke elements—is too important to push off on just anyone. With this direct connection, we have more control over what we're going to get. Our voices remain authentic and consistent, and our fingers are on the pulse to adapt and react as necessary.

THE "FUN" INGREDIENT

Fun is important for the actual diner enjoying a meal, but that fun piece is also important on a macro level, to bring lightness to a business always under intense scrutiny. Restaurants are no longer critiqued by just professionals but casual foodies alike, with voices that can be wide-reaching on social media. Everyone seems to have an opinion about restaurants—and sometimes that's not fun.

But it's all how you take it.

Under the gaze of all these critical eyes, we are determined to do fun things with our food and drink. Embracing the fun lets guests know we're human and we have a sense of humor. Not only do people enjoy the whimsy, but they're often a little more forgiving if something else in the experience falls short. "Fun" takes a lot of different forms in our world.

For a half dozen years, Jeff and I had walked along Thirty-Fifth Street to the glassed-in corner of Growlers Pourhouse. The brick was slowly but always changing as graffiti came and went—Yogi Bear for a while, then Jesus Christ, then a five-foot red rectangle, all coming and going over the original paint that, high up on the building, named a business that had once inhabited the space. In the back corner of the building, at the rear of Growlers Pourhouse, there was a storage closet. The closet was packed tight with equipment, paper products, utensils, and back-up ingredients that, from the inside, hid an arched window looking out onto Thirty-Fifth Street.

We kept looking at the window, thinking of ways we could use it to add a bright spot to our street. With that new intention, the arched window started to appear very different to us. And of course, it wasn't the window itself but rather our perception of it. Haberdish operated a couple doors down with a large basement storage space underneath, so we moved all the junk out of the little closet to clear out the eighty-two-square-foot space. We had a new vision: a walk-up window where we could sell hot, fresh, made-to-order doughnuts. It was tight in there, but we had enough room for one base cake doughnut dressed up in seven daily flavors, along with a seasonal flavor. The inspiration was a doughnut shop Jeff and I had enjoyed in our twenties and thirties on the Jersey Shore.

Because of its size, our shop, Reigning Doughnuts, wouldn't necessarily drive a ton of revenue for us, but it would create new energy on the block. What had been a dark, dingy, somewhat unsafe corner was now lit up with twinkling lights strung over picnic tables. There was one more destination on the street where locals and visitors alike could enjoy a fun foodie experience. They could sit outside and have a fresh-brewed coffee or walk with friends, doughnuts in hand, perusing the strip of shops. They could carry a dozen home to share with their family.

Reigning Doughnuts is fun but not just in its broad concept. In the springtime we've offered a Peep doughnut with a bunny or a chick sticking out of the hole and green icing as a grassy nest. We made an Abominable Snowman doughnut with toasted coconut and little eyeballs. We've mashed up flavors like hot sauce icing with crispy fried chicken skins and done New Year's Eve doughnuts covered in champagne icing with gold sprinkles.

Our "fun" food crosses to our other restaurants too. We have a gorgeous seasonal cocktail at Supperland called the Intergalactic Love Affair, and its beauty and whimsy are apparent as soon as it arrives at your table. The pink drink is topped with a floating purple layer, and edible glitter glints over a strawberry puree ice cube in the shape of a rose. Several cocktails at Haberdish are served over a spherical ice cube that holds a frozen edible flower inside, like it's trapped in a snow globe.

Simple experiential dining ideas are also fun for guests. A heavenly white balsamic mignonette is poured over raw oysters and served alongside our branzino at Ever Andalo. Towering caddies of seafood are eye-catching and delightful. It's exciting when the blackened onion dish continues bubbling at the table and when smoke wafts up from a teapot filled with hot, sizzling butter at Supperland. The simple notion of sharing dishes in a family style environment is fun too. An over-the-top brunch buffet with cinnamon rolls brought to your table feels celebratory and fun.

At Haberdish we took the simple notion of coffee service in a unique, memorable direction. Thinking about the ties between the old textile mills and our restaurant, now a centerpiece in the little neighborhood, we elected to bring coffee to the table in a thermos. Guests can get a whole or a half thermos, and we offer it at the table with coffee cups, cream, and sugar. The thermos is an industrial addition to the table, hearkening to the surrounding former mills, but it's highly experiential just by being different. It's also utilitarian because the coffee stays hot while the guest enjoys lunch or brunch. If it were just coffee in a pot, it's less memorable. A thermos, on the other hand, is added fun.

On a different level, some elements of service may seem boring or mundane, but without them, it's hard for a guest to have fun. It's no fun to be without a serving spoon for your shareable ambrosia salad bowl. It's no fun to have a plate of food that's not hot. It's no fun to not receive the Intergalactic Love Affair cocktail you ordered. It's not fun when you need salt and your server is AWOL. It's not fun when your coffee thermos is brought to your table and there's no cream or sugar. All these things that might be taken for granted in a well-executed service are easily noticed when they're missing.

Eating and entertainment are meshing in the dining environment. Guests are there to eat, yes, but dining is also an interactive form of entertainment. The strategic, intentional creation we work toward is imperative for building out and maintaining relevant dining rooms. If we do it right, the guest's enjoyment is part of the act.

SERVING SPOON: Life doesn't have to just unfold around you—you get to play a part. What thoughtful ideas can you bring to your business or your life to be intentional and directive toward what brings you joy?

Four

EVOLVE

The chemistry of change is delicious.

A prison is a place with closed spaces, little growth, and lots of restrictions. Don't build yourself a prison. That's the biggest piece of advice Jeff and I give to the people who reach out to us about opening their own restaurant, food stall, or food truck. A prison is a place where someone is confined and unable to grow. It is dark, it is lonely, it is not filled with joy—and it is certainly not a place that has room for rising and evolving.

A restaurant prison could look like many things: slumped exhaustion from no rest, no time to recover from the last shift before the next one begins, being on the floor with guests every moment the restaurant is open, running expo to monitor every dish as it leaves the kitchen to make sure it's to spec, completing frantic errands before each shift, or firing someone in the middle of a shift and washing dishes during service because it was the dishwasher who was fired and the dish pit is not the spot to neglect. Prison could look like running solo in the confines of a food truck, grilling up burgers and taco meat and passing them out a window during the heat of summer before feverishly driving up the road with hopes there'll be a good turnout at the Friday movie night at the nearby park. Prison may come five years down the road when the restaurant is putting out the same menu year after year but for a declining guest count.

A prison in the restaurant business is often tethered with mathematics, as we found out in our early days. We only had eleven tables' worth of revenue, and while we had an executive chef, revenue couldn't support a general manager. That meant Jeff was running expo to check dishes over before they left the kitchen, and getting called in when others called out; he was the one fixing toilets and changing light bulbs. It became clear that business growth would spawn flexibility and freedom.

To be clear, there is nothing wrong with being on the service floor every day, or working expo, or manning a food truck, or running the same menu for years *if* it makes you happy. Work isn't a prison when you achieve fulfillment. But if you feel shackled to a concept or a role, you will not evolve to your potential.

Growth can be big or small, but it's still growth. Sometimes we make gigantic strides, like signing a twenty-year lease or buying a restaurant's real estate. Or receiving national recognition and ending up with a new restaurant's name on the cover of *Bon Appétit*. Or cleaning out a storage closet to sell doughnuts out the window as a new revenue stream. Or salvaging a historic building. We hope it means someday getting to when we've paid off all our investors. Those are big steps.

Other times, evolution is more mundane but still critical. A small change may not matter much today, but that small change compounded over a year can make a difference—like raising the price of a single doughnut by twenty cents, adding a touch of miso to give your mac and cheese a more savory flavor, replacing lobster with shrimp on a seafood roll because of the exorbitant price of lobster, reorganizing a space to create room for edible flower garnishes, or adding an additional A/C unit for the comfort of staff and guests. Over a year, the company adjusts and continuously improves through small changes.

Repurposing old buildings wasn't always important to Jeff and me; it became a passion along the way. We didn't intentionally plan to have a growth-mindset work environment, but it became a core value for us as our company grew and we attracted more passionate people to our team. It wasn't always important to us to break out beyond restaurants to do projects like videos or books or speaking, but these have been engaging, positive add-ons to our lives and our businesses. Every day, food must be served—so we have to figure out how to make that happen. And every day, we stay open to what the business can become, knowing that some of the best things are still on the way, and they may arrive entirely by surprise.

We began with a narrow, simple plan: Open a restaurant. In time, though, our vision grew. We evolved. Some of our evolution has been intentional. We planned and created a new concept, and then we opened it. This type of evolution was done with purpose. But the world offers opportunities to evolve anytime change comes along or expectations rise. If we're unable to create new ideas, stay fresh, and keep up, we put our concepts at risk. As the market evolves, technology changes, and culture shifts, so must we. But it's not just about keeping up with these external shifts; as a human being, it's just flat-out rewarding to reach, to achieve, to grow.

DO THE HARD THING

Crêpe Cellar was our first restaurant baby. It was our foray into this business and where we ate dinner every week for years. Our kids grew up enjoying its crêpes, pesto brie fries, and homemade burrata. Hundreds of snapshots from the early days of Crêpe Cellar still flood my mind—that tiny, packed room, dark and candlelit, rolling napkins and bussing tables when I was seven months pregnant and still working another job. It was our first time creating a business and building a team. We would never make another restaurant like it again—founded on a dream, with very few resources, little financial support, and no experience.

In 2019, ten years in, Crêpe Cellar had a stellar year. Jeff and I had occasionally toyed around with the idea of changing the concept to keep fresh in our fast-growing city, but Crêpe Cellar's numbers were off the charts. With strong profits, our first restaurant was still growing. It was time to relax and reap what we had sown.

Fast-forward several months to mid-March 2020, when we were smack in the beginning of COVID and our doors were forced shut. We remained part open, part closed for about a year, with limited hours and all sorts of semi-open situations, from to-go only to partial seating. With a tight dining room, spacing six feet apart was nearly impossible.

Some restaurants, like pizza shops, did pretty well during COVID. Others did okay because they had outdoor seating or wide spaces. Crêpe Cellar did about as poorly as a restaurant could do. Our cozy, intimate experience was, very suddenly, the opposite of what guests were seeking. We were a carcass of a restaurant. Compounding the issue, crêpes don't travel well, so their appeal as a to-go item is limited.

As COVID restrictions were relaxed and we extended our hours, Haberdish recovered well. Supperland opened in March of 2021, and it thrived from the start. Our numbers at Crêpe Cellar, however, lagged, not even coming close to our 2019 levels.

The idea of transforming Crêpe Cellar slowly crept back into our family conversations. It was partly to do with the slower sales, but our team's talent had risen significantly with the opening of Supperland, and our bench was deep with skilled chefs at Haberdish too. It seemed like the time to challenge our incredible team and create something new.

Updating a restaurant is never an easy process. Closing a popular one to create a new concept was a whole other beast, a terrifying risk. We didn't know how guests would react. We didn't know how staff would react, and we risked high employee turnover. Executing an entirely different menu would have challenges with potential new equipment, processes, and needs for refrigeration, freezer space, prep time, and the sauté and fryer areas. Crêpe Cellar and our second restaurant, Growlers Pourhouse, were in a groove putting out two different menus from the same kitchen, so if we scrapped Crêpe Cellar to start fresh, the new menu would still need to thread seamlessly with the Growlers Pourhouse menu.

We also had to consider to what degree we would make changes. Once a space is set up as a restaurant, it can be pretty easy to plunk another one right in its place using the same setup, bathrooms, kitchen layout, equipment, bar, chairs, stools, and tables. It's a ready-made, fully equipped space that needs a new sign and menu. It would have been fairly easy to put a little lipstick on it and open up as a "new" spot. But Jeff and I had bigger things in mind. The ideas wouldn't be cheap or easy to execute, but to successfully launch a new brand to replace one that had been beloved for over a dozen years, the overhaul needed to be bold.

It was just the time to be bold.

In October of 2021, we began to quietly take a new direction for Crêpe Cellar. Days we were closed and slower days became easy times for small construction projects. Between Sundays after brunch and Tuesdays at 5 p.m., we got a lot accomplished in secret. One week we painted the ceiling from black to white. Another week, we ripped up the flooring and put down a custom penny tile pattern in whites, blacks, and light blue. We wrapped the room in siding and, one by one, replaced tabletops with a new stain color. Chairs were swapped out in batches to repaint them black and add a gold embellishment to the back of the seat. When we were low on seats as they got repainted, we borrowed extra chairs from Haberdish to supplement until the paint dried.

About a month into these quiet changes, we sent a press release announcing the full closure of Crêpe Cellar. In part, it read:

> *As a family, we have been touched by how much this place has meant to people over the last 13 years, and we are so grateful to have been a part of our community's lives. We've witnessed proposals, anniversaries, birthdays, first dates, and even "life celebrations" post funerals. It's an honor to get to be a part of all these special moments of life.*
>
> *Closing up has been a difficult decision, but it is also one that is opening the door for us to open Ever Andalo—a concept serving Italian food and wine—and we are SO*

excited for the experience that will come to life there, allowing us to continue to offer a special place for our community. We're also so happy to be able to do this in NoDa—where we have such incredibly loyal, long-time supporters. We're excited to share this new place with everyone!

Sadness poured in as people swallowed the idea that one of their favorite restaurants was never to return. Complaints and comments came next—mainly that we'd never be able to make something better than Crêpe Cellar in that space. We were terrible people to change the concept. Some staff muttered, "If it ain't broke, don't fix it."

It's not easy letting go of something—especially when it is dear to you and integral to your story. But Crêpe Cellar was struggling in ways beyond tangible numbers. Morale was low. Servers weren't making enough in tips to keep them around. Everyone was tired from the laborious battle through the pandemic. Our business needed a refresh, but it needed brave leadership to make it happen. We had to let go if we were going to give that business a chance to thrive again. We saw something better, something invigorating, something to carry our staff along with more secure, better-paying jobs, and something to push cuisine and dining experiences forward in our city. Every business has a lifetime, after all—sometimes it's hundreds of years, sometimes it's forty, and sometimes it's thirteen.

Business swelled as news got out that we were closing. The dining room was booming again, just in time for us to shut down. Our last day as Crêpe Cellar was a Sunday. We opened for brunch and closed at 3 p.m. Jeff, the kids, and I all went that day. A friend gave us flowers at the table, and we lingered long past closing time. The message on the chalkboard read, "Thank you for the last 13 years."

We locked our doors starting that Sunday afternoon for just five weeks to flip the concept to Ever Andalo. The front windows were removed, widened, and replaced with broader, taller, more expansive glass. Wallpaper unrolled to wrap the room in a brightly colored bird pattern with gold Redouté flower prints. Dark green paint covered the siding halfway up the walls. The awnings that had gone up in April 2009, the same ones that had shielded two hundred people as they waited in line for job interviews during the recession, were pulled down. Hanging plants, potted in terra-cotta and bold black and white, were hung from the ceiling, and spunky plants adorned the windowsills. Thin, lacy white curtains draped the windows, bringing a touch of femininity to the industrial openings and heavy world of cars and trucks passing by. The kitchen got an overhaul with organization and equipment, effectively turning a back room into a pasta-making space. We also added a temperature-controlled wine room in a former server station. The space was transformed and ready to launch a new menu, new drinks, and more in-depth service from our front-of-house staff.

In the weeks leading up to the opening of Ever Andalo, the energy of the place shifted. At times more than sixty people crammed inside the small space, determined to hit deadlines. One *Axios* article's headline called it "a manic mad dash to re-open." And it wasn't just our new restaurant's team who showed up. Teammates from across our locations—Haberdish, Growlers Pourhouse, Reigning Doughnuts, and Supperland—chefs, mixologists, and managers came to train, pitch in, and do whatever was needed to pull the new place together.

What neither Jeff nor I knew going into this big change was how much it was going to mean to the people around us. They wanted to be a part of it. They wanted to help make it great. And they did. That place never would have launched so successfully if it hadn't been for the passion, help, time, and energy of the people who showed up—many of them unasked.

The transition was not without its bumps. Some staff stayed; some left to be replaced by eager new faces. There were ups and downs with construction, emotions, public commentary, training, menu development, and even conversations among our team. But on March 3, 2022, 3116 North Davidson Street reopened its doors with a new menu, look, feel, and service.

The Ever Andalo concept was the outcome of Jeff and our three kids gaining Italian citizenship after a ten-year process. The restaurant is a look into Jeff's family roots. There are only a handful of Tonidandels in the US—with the name tracing back to the Dolomites region in northern Italy, where there are hundreds of Tonidandels. One of the villages in that region is called Andalo, and it's the genesis of the name Tonidandel (think: Antonio di Andalo, which eventually became Tonidandel). At Ever Andalo, we serve homemade pastas and breads, antipasti galore, delicious Italian-inspired cocktails, an Italian-only wine list, homemade desserts—and, of course, grappa.

The night we opened, Jeff and I showed up an hour early for team questions and to assist however we were needed. Once service started, we walked from table to table, chatting with our new guests—among them many former Crêpe Cellar regulars—to get feedback and lighten any sadness longtime fans had over shutting down our first restaurant. We were not sad anymore. The energy in the place had elevated to one of hope and optimism.

The dining room was packed with a robust team of front-of-house staff for service and training. Servers were patiently coming and going. Colorful cocktails whisked out to tables, garnished and bright. Steam hovered above freshly plated pastas, and happiness fluttered around the room.

We were there to make sure everything ran smoothly. But we had already hosted several friends-and-family practice nights. Our team had their questions answered. We had trained rigorously and modified our plans for real-time service. The staff was well-armed with a beautiful space, a delicious and flexible menu, and clearly delineated service points to deliver a delightful coursed dining experience.

Jeff and I stepped back to the narrow bathroom hallway, the same place where, thirteen years before, I hid to let out a silent scream of happiness that people had showed up opening night at Crêpe Cellar. They'd shown up despite us not being anyone, despite us not knowing what we were doing, despite it being the recession, despite it only having eleven tables.

I took Jeff's arm and looked over at him. A full dining room at Ever Andalo buzzed on the other side of the hallway's wine racks—now expanded with eighteen tables, a new staff, and brilliant morale. He smiled. It was time for us to go. It was time for our team to rely on one another, to rely on themselves; it was time to find answers, figure out problems, and handle guest requests without us. An hour and a half into our first night of service at Ever Andalo, Jeff and I ducked back through the kitchen, a room fluttering with garnishing, dishwashing, chopping, and frying. We stepped out the back door to a quiet, dark night humming with the sound of southern locusts.

About a mile away, on the very same night, our restaurant toddler, Supperland, was ironically celebrating its first birthday, and we headed there to commemorate a successful year and to honor the bravery it had taken to shut down a fruitful thirteen-year-old restaurant and create something better and more ambitious in its place.

That night at the Supperland chef's counter, we ordered shrimp cocktail, steak, blackened onions, and brussels sprouts. We watched the kitchen from the "front row"—the dance of fire cooking, expo, servers, food-running, and drink-shaking—a real-life celebration of what our team had achieved.

HAPPY "ACCIDENTS"

Sometimes we're very intentional and strategic about making change in our businesses. We're thoughtful, measured, and we study the numbers to put a plan in place that has a high likelihood of positive impact. Other times, growth opportunities come about almost entirely by accident.

"There's no reservation under your name tonight." Uh-oh.

It was a Wednesday night, and I had reservations at Supperland for three people at 6:45 p.m.—or so I thought. Supperland has no room for walk-ins around 7 p.m., even for the owner. My friends and I didn't have any options, so we modified the plan and found a first come, first serve table at the Supperland bar just across the patio in our smaller building. We usually had some tables for seating at the bar, but we didn't serve our full dining room menu—just bar bites. Still, at least we could have something!

When we sat down, since we had a reservation mix-up, our server offered for us to order from the full menu not just the bar bites menu.

Now, this might seem a little strange: I'm the owner; of course I *could* order whatever I want. But Jeff and I never want to burden the restaurants—ours is the order that gets pushed back if we're in the "weeds" or way behind in service. In addition, since we opened our bar, it had been challenging for the kitchen to do the full menu in both the dining room and bar. It's a lot of fire cooking to keep up with, the bar is in a separate building, plus our bartenders were never fully trained on the same service points as in the main dining room. I never want to put any of our staff out during a busy service by making unnecessary requests.

Hunger won.

My friends and I accepted the full menu, ordering a seafood tower, sliced steak, smashed potatoes, and some wood-fired vegetables. The service was surprisingly smooth, the food was hot, everything was timely, and the bartender brought silverware, serving spoons, and tongs similar to what we bring guests in the main dining room.

That happy accident (not having a reservation) led to a flood of conversations about why we don't ordinarily serve the full menu at the bar, since the team had settled in after solid years in the business. Knowing our revenue numbers, our main dining room was crushing it for dinner, whereas our bar food menu was never a big traffic driver. If our full menu could be served at the bar, we could invite main dining room walk-ins to enjoy our food in our bar space rather than our main dining room, which could make a huge difference for the bar's revenue and allow us to serve more walk-in guests.

Ironically, we had spent several tastings and many hours developing a new bar bites menu, but that week, we pivoted. Only a couple months later, the full menu started up at the bar, and it had an immediate impact on nightly sales. It was the growth we needed as we moved through another year of operations, and it came about from leaning into an "accident."

Creating change is rarely straightforward. There are stops and starts, cruises and adventures, jams and accidents. While business growth is often a go-go-go process, there are always opportunities if you pause and look around—and stay on your toes for how to use the situation to your advantage. Those "accidents" that inevitably pop up in business, when capitalized upon, may contain a treasure trove of ways to find still more growth.

EVOLVE THE BIZ

Handcrafted focaccia requires careful preparation to achieve the inherent malleability and adaptability of the bread. It's a little spongy, a little soft, drags nicely through olive oil, and provides a great base for toppers like olives or red onions or goat cheese. At Ever Andalo our pastry team mixes up the focaccia dough with a kneading hook. The dough rests. We then pour the dough into circular springform pans that cover a large counter. A chef pokes finger holes into each loaf, dimpling the dough in random patterns. A drizzle of olive oil over each adds a yellow-greenish hue and holds the sprinkle of salt that follows. After another rest, the focaccia goes into the ovens daily.

Served with a rosemary sprig, the bread steams when you pull it apart or drag the serrated knife through it. On our bread board, we serve a small pile of Maldon's Sea Salt and that three-compartment dish with a DOP olive oil flight sourced from various parts of Italy. We don't get that delicious end product without the time that the bread rests, allowing it to rise and develop air pockets, and giving it a soft, airy texture. Without that time, the bread would bake up like a stiff, thick cracker.

Focaccia's softness and flexibility are the keys to long-term persistence and growth. Like the bread, we must be open to new ideas and ways of doing things. During rising time, there's growth and expansion. If you don't take time for this process, the business will be like that stiff, thick cracker: unyielding. There's no fluidity to advance. But once you elevate your business, there's a moment to settle in and steady yourself before it's time to reach for the next change.

Success in the restaurant business depends on continual assessment and ongoing learning. Our diverse team serving a diverse clientele thrives when it's nimble, adroit, and eager to learn. Continuous learning has always been part of Jeff's and my personal life, which makes it a natural core value for our business culture—an essential one too. But learning isn't just about acquiring knowledge. It's about opening your heart toward change and growth.

In our neighborhood, gigantic pin oaks hang high in the sky. "Be like the tree," I whisper to myself while gawking at the lush canopy. The looming giants are a sight. But it's not their size that enthralls me. The tiniest sprigs captivate me, too, jutting up from patches of moss, with their bud-like golden tips. Large or small, they grow effortlessly. Plants don't think about what time of year it is or the time of day. They don't decide when to flower or when to produce fruit or seeds. They don't try at anything. They sit still as life force flows through them and nature takes its course. The tree grows and rings accumulate. The moss thickens then sprouts dancing stems. Without effort, they grow.

We humans often tend toward wrangling and forcing things to happen wherever, whenever, and however we want them to. There's treasure in going after things with passion and pointedness—but there's also balance in allowing, making way for more "being" and less "doing." Plants lack resistance. They accept. With that allowance, life happens.

Most humans want to grow, too, just like plants, but we're typically after intellectual, spiritual, and emotional growth, not just the physical. The desire to grow and learn is rampant in our teammates, many of whom are young or unsure of what they want to achieve in life. We see immense opportunity in helping them rise.

Early on in our restaurant beginnings, Colleen Hughes came to work with us as a server and bartender. At first we expected that, like most servers, she would be here for a while and then go. But she took an interest in beer, its unique flavors and ways of bringing out those flavors when making the beer. Her attention then shifted to cocktails and the intricate nuances between types of liquors and the flavor components that create a balanced, well-delivered drink. Colleen's hunger for knowledge was clear. She had found her passion in creating craft cocktails.

Jeff and Colleen found various conferences and learning opportunities to establish her expertise, and she took advantage of all of them. Though she started with little experience, Colleen created her path by being open, by absorbing information, and by taking advantage of the opportunities in front of her. She is now the head mixologist across our restaurants, creating flavorful, thoughtful, beautiful drinks for each of them. Her talents and hard work have positioned her as a James Beard nominee as well.

With her reach across our bar programs, Colleen has been integral in creating growth for our teammates too. We host regular training sessions for our team to learn about bourbon or gin or making classic cocktails, so each bartender increases in proficiency. Bartenders sprinkled throughout the city have trained under Colleen, and their opportunities have grown because of the knowledge she passed along and because of the reputation a place like Supperland or Haberdish has earned in the Charlotte cocktail scene.

Education is a key component in the success of our business. Our team is made up of people who adore food—and its accompanying elements of drink, hospitality, and generosity. These individuals crave knowledge about the industry. Many don't just want a job; they want something fulfilling. Education helps bridge that gap. Education and its sister, experience, expand the mind with new ideas and approaches, and thoughts begin to connect in unexpected ways.

During one educational session, one of our suppliers brought in twenty different kinds of microgreen garnishes. Across the tables at Supperland, small piles of greens were placed on trays with the names of each one written in marker underneath. Some of the garnishes were aimed at providing texture to a dish. Others could offer contrasting colors for visual appeal, and still others would add layered, subtle flavor notes to the dish. There were piles of wispy greens and wider yellow petals, there were pansies and bull's blood, arugula sprouts and organic edible flowers still attached at the stem. We sniffed to sense notes of lemongrass or bitterness or pepper. Other pinches we'd taste in nibbles, trying to decipher how the microgreens could bring out the intrinsic flavor of an item on our menu and, in the process, broaden chefs' minds.

With the help of one of our liquor partners, we sent bartenders to Kentucky to learn about bourbon. Gathered around a barrel, the team ladled up tastes and learned about the history of the spirit. Our team even developed a barrel of their own choice. Back here in Charlotte, we offer a one-of-a-kind spirit—the outcome of the travels and insights of our team members who journeyed to Kentucky.

When liquor reps come in to teach our staff about a spirit such as gin, often anyone on our team is invited. The reps talk about the history of the beverage and the brand they represent, then there's an in-depth tasting. With subtleties from one liquor to the next, ideas exchange for pairings or mixed drinks. Our staff is engaged. They get opportunities to learn. Some of them get ideas for cocktail development too.

We ran a three-session leadership training program for thirty of our managers over the course of several months. We've purchased cookbooks to help inspire a teammate's passion even more. Other times, we take our executive chefs out to dinner at new restaurants. We've also taken chefs to Chicago, Miami, New York, Atlanta, and California, with the help of our primary food supplier, Gordon Foods, for learning opportunities and restaurant visits.

We've set up sustainable, ongoing processes that facilitate improvements in our business too. One of the most notable is our weekly tastings. At a tasting, the chefs are given specific items to test or an open slate to present new ideas. Chefs show up with notes, ingredients, and cooking processes to explain how a dish was made and its intent. Together, we assess how the dish might fit in with the brand or specials at that particular restaurant or for an upcoming event.

Taking time for tastings maintains quality, but tastings also generate continuous improvement—and that's growth. Our tastings at Ever Andalo led to a change from tortellini to tortelloni (more on this change later). We've discovered new dishes, like Haberdish's drool-worthy champagne-battered chicken tenders. Tastings have uncovered weak links in our processes, like when we learned that our tomatoes at Ever Andalo were getting put in the food processor for too long, making the sauce thin like SpaghettiOs sauce. Creative doughnut flavors spawn out of tastings—from caramel popcorn to blackberry pie, avocado chocolate drizzle, and even a lox doughnut. Gorgeous boba-topped intermezzos came out of tastings. Our seasonal dishes run through our tasting days, and that keeps our menu ideas fresh and packed with local farm produce.

Beyond these business practices, each year, Jeff and I travel to places we've never been. Of course, we go to restaurants, and our eyes are on hypersearch, taking in everything from the spacing on a menu to lapels of the servers, from table bases to bill inserts, pens, unique pour-overs, napkin folds, glassware, and light bulbs. But we're also looking at the ways experiences unfold all around us outside of restaurants: the unusual color of a street sign, the ease in the methodology for mobile app parking, the types of flowers in a flower box, the way we're greeted at a store's front desk, the manner in which coffee is brought to a hotel room, the contrast in design colors, upholstery choices, even flooring and doorway architecture.

Inspiration bubbles up from so many places, and it helps to look at these different, unconnected sensory experiences and how they may combine. Sometimes our improvements are as simple as adding revenue streams—a retail component for merchandise, a brunch, a happy hour, a wine event—all things that continuously evolve and improve our business. Other times it's seeing a different business, like a spa, and how a simple thing like steamy towels at the end of a meal can enhance a dining experience. Unexpected surprises, like a hot towel at the end of a meal, have ways of bringing out smiles or memorable exchanges as the meal closes. Some guests elect not to use the towels, but I've also witnessed a fifty-year-old woman cover her whole face with the towel and caress her cheeks softly in glee. While unconventional, the towel added to her experience.

To remain relevant, openness to change is imperative. That's about having openness to all the inspiration around you, but it's also about having constructs and systems that continuously encourage your business to keep fresh, evolve, learn, and create.

PATIENCE WITH EVOLUTION

One day in early spring 2022, as I was walking around my neighborhood, it occurred to me that part of my evolving job was to create a pipeline of projects for our company. It was right up my alley—seeing potential in things. In a city where a lot of old buildings were ripped down to make room for the new, I could seek out projects to excite us and allow us to use old spaces in new ways.

I'm looking for a compelling new restaurant project, I whisper to myself, in my new self-proclaimed business development role. Hands on the grocery cart, filling up with arugula, shiitakes, limes, and bananas: *I'm looking for a compelling new restaurant project*. At the gym, hoisting ten-pounders over my head or on long walks under the lofty oaks in my neighborhood: *I'm looking for a compelling new restaurant project*. To and from soccer, tennis, and dance. Whisper, whisper: *I'm looking for a compelling new restaurant project*.

Later that week, driven by my mantra, I got in my car and revved up. Surely if I drove around town, I would come across something. My wheels took me all over the west side of Charlotte. I drove into little Belmont. I drove through Plaza Midwood and farther east, down Central Avenue. I drove south and north, and I continued my search online, looking for interesting old buildings, somewhere to call home for our next concept to follow our most recent concepts, Supperland and Ever Andalo. I spent eight hours in the car that week. Nothing surfaced.

About two weeks later, my friend shared a rumor that a nearby restaurant building was being sold to a local celebrity who had the ambition to open an art gallery. It was a mere four blocks from our house, it was a former church building, and it was in our charming Dilworth neighborhood with the booming growth of South End just one block in another direction.

Other than our deep-rooted fears of opening a restaurant in Dilworth, Jeff and I would have loved that site for a project. But we were too late. And despite having sworn years before that we'd never again try to open a restaurant in Dilworth, I couldn't stop thinking about that spot. There were so many things to love about the building. The 1915 church with all the dings and stories and character that came along with those hundred-plus years was close to home. The site had been operating as a fine-dining restaurant called Bonterra for twenty-two years, so Jeff and I knew a restaurant buildout was feasible. Also, we already had one restaurant, Supperland, in a church. Why not a second? I visited Bonterra's social media for clues about their planned closure and relocation to another neighborhood. I found nothing significant, but at the top of the restaurant's feed was a photo of a man holding out a plate of food. In the background was a very familiar figure. I looked closer. It was Jeff. The photo had been taken during an event three years prior, but it had curiously been posted just two days before. *Was I looking for that building, or was it looking for me?*

"It's a sign!" I screamed at Jeff from the couch. "It's a sign we should reach out to them."

The next day, Jeff reached out to the realtor to express interest. The call confirmed that the property was indeed being sold to that local celebrity as an art gallery. Jeff closed the conversation and gave them our information just in case anything went awry. Five months passed, and I kept looking for our next spot, but I didn't forget about that one. Despite it already having a purchaser, I didn't want to let go of the idea. Then one day, the realtor called. The other deal had fallen through. The owner would give us one week to pull the financing together before putting it out to the public. It was a scramble and a near fumble when our first loan option didn't go through, but we got the property.

My twin sister, Kerry, was our first investor at Crêpe Cellar, and while she didn't have a lot of money to give at the time, she believed in us and in our dream. Recently I asked Kerry what she considered the most notable reason for our success to date. Her answer surprised me: patience.

Patience isn't a glamorous virtue. When done right, it's unnoticed. But Jeff and I wouldn't have gotten where we are without it.

Acquiring the Bonterra building taught me the role of patience when you believe in something. Reality needs time to catch up to the dream, but belief in where I want to go is my North Star. Just because something isn't in front of me straightaway doesn't mean it's not worth fighting for. Things won't necessarily pan out the way I expect they will, but it is almost always better than I'd anticipated. I've learned to wait. The product of evolution and the manifestation of dreams takes time.

SERVING SPOON: What can you do today to allow yourself or your business to change? What can you be more open to? Change within compels change outside of you too.

Five

PERSIST

Building beautiful flavors takes time.

Everyone in the restaurant industry gets smacked around from time to time. It's a tough business with a lot of critical eyes and thousands of things that can go wrong every day. We're in a labor-intensive business, and one that relies on hundreds of people to do their part (hello, farmers, delivery trucks, linen companies, beer line cleaners, wine reps, servers, bartenders, dishwashers, chefs, food runners). People also often treat restaurant workers like the "help," and they forget manners and general kindness. Sometimes guests outright take stuff off our tabletops, thinking they're a souvenir of some kind. Then there are the reviews—some with merit, some not—but we have to face them either way.

We grow thicker skin. We learn to get up and try again. We take feedback and improve. We open our hearts toward greater hospitality and grace. We get up the next day and do it all over again.

TAKE THE HEAT

Since we've been in the business, labor has been a challenge. Servers make nearly twice as much as many hourly back-of-house teammates—teammates who work behind the scenes in the kitchen, making all the food, even delivering the food to the table. This includes cooks, porters, dishwashers, and food runners. Our front-of-house teammates—hosts, managers, bartenders, servers, and server assistants—relate with guests, make food and drink suggestions, and provide an environment of hospitality and fun. Because of the way restaurants are currently permitted to pay employees based on whether they are tipped or not tipped, the discrepancy between pay and pay potential is different between these two separate but codependent groups.

When our menu prices increase, servers are happy because their tips grow, but this does nothing for the back-of-house workers. No matter how organically we grow or how much more food we put out each year, our kitchen staff doesn't reap the benefits instantaneously. They work harder to put out more food, but they are paid a flat rate. If the business does very well, we're able to provide some wage increases to our lowest-paid back-of-house workers. But because of tipping, servers see an immediate impact on their paychecks. With servers getting a raise every time we raise our prices, this disparity between front and back of house will just keep growing.

Turnover is commonplace in the restaurant industry. A server job or bartending job is often a side gig. In the front of house, we've hired a lot of part-time teachers, students, artists, and musicians—they are with us to earn money while they follow a personal passion. People come and go, and many don't think of the restaurant business as a viable career choice. Many servers simply "age out." When they're ready to settle down with a family, the restaurant lifestyle no longer suits them. In the back of house, a lot of turnover is a result of how busy our kitchens are. Workers can get a job in a slower kitchen and earn the same salary or hourly rate with time to relax between orders.

The predictability of turnover doesn't make it easier to stomach. We lose a lot of time, energy, and money when a trained staff member leaves us. This industry is competitive—more so now than ever—and people leave because of new restaurant openings, growth opportunities for higher-level positions, or even a job that promises just fifty cents more per hour.

Labor has always been a challenge, and it is also the cost segment of our business that has been the most volatile. We have many people who show up every day and give us their best; they're passionate about hospitality and food and taking care of guests. But because restaurant jobs aren't everyone's passion, we can have issues with poor attitudes, which leads to problems with camaraderie, timeliness, positivity, and quick turnover after investing in training. With hundreds of people on our team, negativity can impact the culture of a restaurant, including the guest experience.

The restaurant industry has shifted with workplace expectations too. Most changes are positive overall, but even change for the better can be difficult to implement, especially for longtime industry teammates. Some people aren't open to making a change that others are ready to run with. For example, we have some teammates eager to embrace self-selected pronoun use, while others do not even understand the notion—they grew up differently, and it's challenging to change learned language norms. Age differences matter; old-school kitchen workers may have become accustomed to a hard-driven, bullying environment, one that doesn't pause to consider people's feelings. We now have a more even gender balance in our kitchens and a wide range of age groups, and our culture is lighter and more open-minded. Chefs have to evolve in empathy and not be angry jerks who throw things, or they get shown the door. Kitchens are slowly becoming friendlier places to work—but change is still change, and a diverse group of individuals will accept it in a diverse range of ways.

Despite the industry's many challenges on the labor front, our business has worked through bit by bit, taking each issue as it comes and facing it head-on. We've found the stormy business climate to be a little like surfing. Gigantic waves of change crush or drown businesses every day—but with a little flexibility and patience, those same waves can be the very reason you coast gracefully to shore.

It was March 16, 2020, around 11 a.m., when we got word that our restaurants would all have to close due to COVID-19. None of us knew what was coming, but by noon, Jeff had told every teammate at Haberdish we had to let them go. He walked down to Crêpe Cellar, Growlers Pourhouse, and Reigning Doughnuts and did the same thing.

Analyzing what other restaurants around the country were doing, we determined one plan of action, and we quickly opened a walk-up window to serve to-go orders from our kitchens. A smaller menu would compile favorites from Crêpe Cellar, Growlers Pourhouse, and Reigning Doughnuts. By opening the window, we would run through the product our team had already prepped and keep food waste in check. Then, moving forward, the menu could just include our bestsellers—a hodgepodge of crêpes, doughnuts, and sandwiches—to keep ingredients down and make it doable by hiring a handful of kitchen staff back to our team. We created a name for this new pop-up concept: Bring the Queen. Charlotte is the Queen City, after all, and considering the circumstances, we all could have used a queen to navigate the unprecedented situation. But of course, there was no queen coming—we had to be our own queen.

Once we conceived the plan, I arrived at the back door of Crêpe Cellar. I punched in my code. It was the middle of the day, but it was eerily quiet. The kitchen was clean and still. No sounds of pots clanking or dishes stacking, no fryer bubbling. I snaked my way to the dining room and past the bar. The front of house was just as quiet, the lights off. Empty tables devoid of silverware and napkins were a reminder that no one would be walking through our doors anytime soon.

At the front wall, six-top booths lined the windows. For a moment I stood still, taking it all in, wondering how we had gotten where we were. I stepped forward. The far window looked like a great spot for a to-go order staging area.

I dragged the two sides of the banquette away from the window to create room. I swept out the area under the windowsill—dust and small food bits and children's crayons filled the dustpan. Around the edges of the window, I wiped out grime, then raised the window to clean out the nooks and crevices surrounding the glass. Outside, street dust covered the white siding, but it would shine after an hour of wiping and scraping. I placed a potted plant from inside, outside the window on a stool. A small chalk-board sign now read "Bring the Queen Pick-Up Window."

We battled like so many restaurants did during COVID. It wasn't pretty, it wasn't glamorous, and in a lot of ways, we didn't get anywhere. Bring the Queen wasn't a success—not in terms of profitability, anyway, but we tried. We paddled our little ship as hard as we could in a rough storm. It kept our minds forward-thinking. It provided a couple of kitchen jobs. And maybe it gave a little hope to our neighborhood, city, and team that things would shape up again someday. In this business, with the number of things that can go wrong each day, grit is the only option. Whether ongoing labor issues or a worldwide pandemic, no one is coming to save you—surely not the queen. It's up to you to take the heat and keep on.

LET GO

Everyone has an opinion, especially in the restaurant world. Sometimes it's about flavor: more smoke, less paprika, too creamy, not enough butter, too much salt. Sometimes it's how a dish is cooked: underdone, overdone, too crispy, too soft. The opinions go beyond the tabletop too. From light-ing levels to the comfort of chairs to the difficulty of getting a reservation and the personality of a specific server, opinions run the gamut. People complain about a crowded restaurant and the noise that accompanies that full room—and they complain if there are a lot of open tables when they dine at 4:30 p.m. We only take credit cards at our walk-up-window doughnut shop, and we've heard a variety of opinions on being a cashless business. The temperature of any restaurant also gets a lot of action: too hot, too cold, too humid, too anything.

The number of ways to complain about a restaurant is limitless, and they're all subjective. During the pandemic, it all got worse. The complaints were so grating, so cutting, and all over the board. One day, we had a complaint come in on social media degrading our whole team and calling us "super spreaders." Later that same day, guests stormed out of our restau-rant, calling us "woke" because our staff continued to wear masks at their discretion after the mask mandate had ended. We aim toward what's best for our staff. Our team works inside our doors with hundreds of visitors pouring through every night. We leave it to them to make individual decisions about what makes them feel safe.

If our teammates have done everything they can to remedy a difficult situation and we've been open to learning how to handle a matter next time, we move on. When we can't appease an angry guest, we have no choice but to brush it off and move forward with positivity. As Ted Lasso says to Sam Obisanya in *Ted Lasso*, "Be a goldfish." Simply: forget.

In the first year we opened Ever Andalo, we received a terrible review. In over a decade of being in the business, it was the worst review we'd received for any restaurant. Pressure was high to succeed after having closed down the popular Crêpe Cellar, and the review of Ever Andalo was embarrassing and way off track from where we aimed to be. While I muddled through the full review, Jeff wouldn't read it.

"I'm not listening to them," he said. "We have room to improve, but we know what we're doing." He's always been better at closing his ears off to the world around him and keeping his eyes on our vision.

Given the fragility of our new restaurant, this review, left unaddressed, could have shaken our team. Instead, we looked for an opportunity and posted an internal note to our staff from Jeff:

> *Hey all, in the wake of the rather scathing review, I just wanted to encourage everyone to keep their chins up. Poor reviews happen, and they do not define us. This team is doing an excellent job. Every day. There will always be things to work through, and we will glean out the constructive feedback to make ourselves better. We will, however, not change our love for this place, the people who come here, the dishes we make, the ingredients we bring in, and the love we have for the guests we serve just because of a negative review.*
>
> *I love this menu and what we have ALL put together— this is an outstanding restaurant, and it is only improving.*

I'm grateful to every one of you for all the efforts. Let's see this only as a springboard for even better times ahead. Thank you!

With a new staff and new culture under construction, this was a pivotal moment. In the face of what some might have seen as a disgrace, we let the incident serve as a teaching moment. Our food got better. Our service improved. We hadn't reached perfection, but we had a vision of what we wanted. We got there. Ever Andalo continues to do double (sometimes triple) the revenue of Crêpe Cellar. It is buzzy, fun, delicious, and well-loved. It was also selected by Yelp as the #8 Best New Restaurant in the country in 2023—a rating based on the number of reviews and star ratings of reviews. We weren't the only ones who loved our new concept.

Even if we didn't receive favorable accolades for Ever Andalo, the lesson for us was about letting go of what others say and steadfastly pursuing our vision, despite it feeling far off. The outside world doesn't dictate our path. We have the power to choose another direction. Always.

TWEAK RECIPES

Persisting in this business has taken a lot of shapes for us individually and as a company, and sometimes it is just a small tweak—looking at something in a different way—that allows us to keep forging along.

Supperland—like Haberdish—is uniquely woven into its space. Our vision was an intentional departure from the average steakhouse. We wanted to give a modern take on the old-fashioned boy's club steakhouse. The menu offers steaks, seafood, and a whole chicken, all served family style. Beautiful flames dance in our open show kitchen as grilled vegetables, porridge bread, and whole fish are garnished for guests.

Despite its creation being during the mire of COVID, there is nothing sobering about Supperland. It's grand. It's brightened by delicate flowered wallpaper. The plates are custom designed; the tables are handmade. Every bit of the place is curated and intentional. Jeff and I made this restaurant an expression of joy and gratitude, offering to guests the best we had within us—even during a difficult time.

For the first two years we operated Supperland, we only served dinner. Filled with the jovial conviviality of celebrations, the place enlivened from the crackles of the first sparks of fire, through the forkfuls, smiles, pops of champagne, and smoke drifts of blown-out birthday candles. Each table of guests as they came and went offered salubrious energy into the grand room, contagiously shared by the people around them. As our two-year anniversary arrived, we stepped back to ponder what growth at the celebratory Supperland could be: What would it look like to use our space during the day? Could we create a luxurious daytime service to draw people in earlier?

Our first thought was a welcoming, high-end afternoon tea menu.

Understanding the vision, our pastry chef, Savannah Foltz, presented Jeff and me a plate of perfectly rectangular tea sandwiches on a spongy white bread with soft edges. Crisp cucumbers topped the shapes in layers of circles with creamy herbed cheese in between. There were pimento cheese sandwiches, too, shingled in triangles and served with a sweet onion jam. A plate of warm mini scones followed, freshly baked with bits of apricot poking from the crusty tops—with clotted cream, of course. With these delicate menu items in mind, we scoured the internet for all the cute tea utensils. We were swept away with the idea—but just for a time. As fitting as offering a ritzy, colorful, delicious afternoon tea was, we allowed the discussion to shift. We reconsidered. What if we could do *anything*? Was there something we were missing that would be bolder and more lucrative, to make a big impact and not just be a small boost to sales? How could we tweak our idea for greater impact?

We knew our restraints. Dinner service was covered, so whatever we did would have to fit earlier in the day. Meals earlier in the day are typically capped at between $20 and $30 per person at a high-end spot. Our Supperland guests spend $90 to $100 each for dinner service. Whatever we did in the earlier hours would need to be worthy of not only upholding our high Supperland experience standards but also building upon them. Ultimately, we decided that Supperland would offer a weekend brunch buffet, one that would include some of the touches we'd been considering for afternoon tea.

Buffets can conjure up thoughts of gluttony, greed, overeating, and a wide spread of scoop-and-serve food plopped onto plates. On birthdays when I was little, my grandparents used to take us for dinner at the Ponderosa cafeteria buffet for mashed potatoes drowning in thick brown gravy, biscuits with those perfectly square pats of butter, and semiprocessed turkey breast shingles in a deep pan. I loved it.

Then on certain Sundays, to celebrate a special occasion, my family dined at the country club. Tables brimmed with piles of chocolate-covered strawberries with speckles of powdered sugar and jelly-filled pastries in flaky round and square crusts. A tall-hatted chef manned a carving station, where he sliced a steaming roast and topped it with warm gravy. Colorful fruit striped a long table, and lettuces in an array of greens were followed by bright red tomatoes, cubed cucumber, bright orange cheese, and small buckets with labels for Thousand Island, French, and ranch dressings. An omelet station offered pink cubed ham, shredded cheese, green onions, and bacon bits to add to your eggs. Steamy knotted breads with bits of garlic hid under a cloth napkin. The food at the country club buffet made an impression, but so did the simple grandeur.

The brunch buffet at Supperland couldn't just be about delicious food and endless visits to a buffet. We'd make great food, but our guests needed grandeur, too, the whole meal and experience orchestrated for their enjoyment. We had one major obstacle: Our restaurant wasn't designed to host a buffet. With long, narrow walkways for seating and a relatively small space for our buffet, the brunch was heading toward lengthy lines, a congested middle area, and frustrated guests.

We couldn't let that happen.

Over multiple run-throughs, meetings, and practice days, we devised an intimate brunch that combined a hearty buffet with a unique touch of table service. The three-stationed buffet lined up across our chef's counter with a spot for frittata; one for skewered filet, shrimp, and vegetables; and another station for made-to-order eggs Benedict. At the stations, several other dishes like brussels sprouts, bacon, homemade sausage, and grits with gravy were served. Having these stations allowed guests to line up at each station instead of across a long buffet line. That kept down wait times for food.

In the middle of the dining room, a large, clothed table took up a portion of the middle aisle to present lobster deviled eggs, strawberries and cream, salads, fresh pastries, and dessert bites. This table could be approached from all sides—with plates stationed strategically—also keeping long lines at bay. The last element of the buffet really set it apart. Several items, including chilled seafood and homemade iced cinnamon rolls, would be brought directly to the tables. Guests didn't have to get up for these tableside dishes, keeping people in seats for longer periods of time—increasing the enjoyment of the meal and keeping our lines in check.

We're also very particular with the way we greet guests at the table for our Supperland brunch. It is super specific and meticulously tested—and it's done to give optimal hospitality. We can't take drink orders or explain to the group how the buffet works if half the table is already up at the buffet and milling about the desserts. We need to debrief them on the experience up front to communicate all the details so both the guest and our team are set up for the buffet.

As a result, when a guest is seated, we first welcome them with charred pineapple with citrus hot honey. Second, our team member takes drink orders—being sure to address specific coffee or tea requests (milk, cream, oat milk, sugar, honey, etc.). Third, we explain the buffet options, including the items staff serve at the chef's counter (our hot items), what's brought directly to the table for guests, and the highlights at our center buffet table. It isn't until each of these topics is covered in that initial greeting that the server leaves the table. It's a lot to cover all at once, but it sets up every guest to enjoy the buffet at their leisure.

In practice days, prior to opening the buffet brunch, we struggled terribly with food quality issues. During each of our early test days, food temperature was inconsistent. Raw oysters came out lukewarm. Grilled prime steak skewers were drying out and not holding heat. Brussels sprouts were cool by the time we got back to our tables.

We made significant changes. Raw oysters moved to a small metal tray with ice—two half shells in each. For the steak skewers, we cut larger pieces that would stay moist and retain a medium-rare cook. We also reduced the skewer batch sizes so they wouldn't sit out as long and added heat lamps to supplement the induction burners sitting underneath the skewers. Our brussels sprouts worked similarly. With both a heat lamp and an induction warmer working, we also shifted to smaller batches of sprouts. Staff learned to stir the pot to move the sprouts around the pan to warm them up. When scooping onto a plate, the team pulled from the bottom, where the sprouts were warmer. Small adjustments made an incredible difference to the quality of the food and service.

Beyond food, practice-day tweaks for brunch ran the gamut: Deliver teacups to the table with a petite demi spoon and include an explanation of the tea timer, specific tea steep times, and the way the unusual honey pot pours from the bottom. Wipe all buffet plates before stacking them to catch any less-than-spotless plates. Bring in silicone spoons so we don't scrape our enameled pans. Order extra high chairs for all the families now joining us at brunch with little ones. Soak skewers so they don't burn on the grill. Don't allow food runners to offer passed items to a table until the charred pineapple is in place, cuing that the server has completed the initial greet.

The number and depth of details was extraordinary, and every adjustment guaranteed we were giving our guests better hospitality. It took a lot of effort, trial and error, and willingness to improve, but it brought about an incredible dining experience for our guests.

Our guests never see the intricate setup effort that happens every Saturday and Sunday to make that buffet possible. With a cart that rolls out of our downstairs riser room, the servers bring out baskets, sneeze guards, linens, and sets of shelves. Dried flowers in large vases are carried up the stairs and displayed on the buffet table, and signage for every item is set out on golden stands. Linens are steamed. Three-tiered displays are set up. Every detail is stowed in that downstairs closet, and it's unpacked and reboxed every service. We paddle like maniacs to make it happen, but to the guest, it's a chill weekend brunch with all the details handled.

Brunch at Supperland added about $1 million to our yearly revenue. This opportunity came about simply because we stepped back to look at our business and the space in a different way. It was a carefully measured decision. We didn't want a greedy, quick-table-turn buffet. We didn't want long lines of frustrated people. We didn't want a cheap $20/person breakfast spot. We anticipated that people would gladly pay for excellent service, high-quality food, fabulous beverages, and a difficult-to-replicate experience. We guessed right. Our team battled innumerable challenges, but we kept at it. We persisted. We kept tweaking and adjusting the little things. Now, each Saturday and Sunday, we seat approximately 150 people to enjoy the bounty and luxuriousness of the Supperland buffet.

SWAY

Tall buildings have room to sway. Same thing with bridges—they aren't completely static. They're built to withstand large temperature swings and high winds. It seems scary to think these towering objects don't stand perfectly still, but if they did, their structure would be at risk. Like a willow tree, they can withstand some movement so they don't crack.

In a high-pressure business, or any business, that flexibility and sway can help you persist through difficulties. We constantly have to stay alert to any changes going on in the broader industry or within our individual restaurant doors so we can react quickly and strategically. Flexibility allows for quick, spontaneous decisions.

When a fire at Haberdish took down one of our main ovens, making it inoperable, we obtained used equipment from a closed-down restaurant to bridge the time until we fixed the burned oven. We jumped on that issue within the day and were open that night for service. When last-minute cancellations in our ten-seat Supperland speakeasy mean eight out of ten people are no longer coming, we invite friends or teammates or influencers to enjoy the planned experience so the room feels fun and full for the couple of guests who could join us. If an apartment above our space complains about noise, we seek noise-dampening solutions so we're operating responsibly in our neighborhood. When the cost of an item on our menu makes it no longer profitable, we act quickly so it doesn't drain our food costs and have time to impact our overall profit. It either gets removed or replaced, depending on whether we've got something to go in its spot. If the ingredient is critical for operations, we modify our offering to make it work.

The price of limes, for instance, spiked upward in the early 2020s. Limes are key for some of our food menu items, but especially key on our cocktail menus. We sell a lot of cocktails on a daily basis, so a simple ingredient or garnish like citrus can have a surprisingly large effect financially. We jumped on a few changes. We stopped putting limes on waters or soda waters unless a guest requested one. Next, we modified our lime cut to a narrower slice, reducing the size of each wedge. In the prep for our cocktails—which is typically entirely homemade—we supplemented recipes with store-bought lime juice. Last, we adjusted our cocktail menus, moving away from margaritas for a time until prices got back in line.

Similarly, during the start of the pandemic, we were using a certain brand of doughnut mix. A few months into the pandemic, that brand was struggling with sourcing, so we switched to a different mix. Of course, every other doughnut shop in the country did the same thing, and very quickly, Brand 2's mix went out of stock too. That left us with one option: to make the mix ourselves. That's when the big wins came in. Jeff started with research, talked with our pastry chef, and then spent a day making different renditions of the mix. That effort changed our course. To this day, we continue to make our own mix. Not only is it cheaper for us, but it also allows us to use fresher, whole ingredients—like real eggs, real milk, flour, and vanilla. Before, it was just a powdered mix. Our new, homemade mix actually lasts about an hour in service, whereas the bagged mix lasted only about thirty-five minutes. Our "sway" conveniently resulted in a better outcome in both the short- and long-term.

We had similar struggles with sourcing liquor during the pandemic, and while a lot of bars went without inventory, limiting and modifying their menus, we sent a bartender in their car driving all over town to find liquors to stock our bars. At the time, we were selling $50K in cocktails across our places, and that loss would have been big. We got someone on the road quickly, and as a result, people continued to frequent our bars because we had the liquor to serve them. When the power went out at one restaurant, we got a team to move as much food to one of our other restaurants' walk-in refrigerators as possible. When the doughnut machine went down for two weeks because we couldn't source parts, we shifted to selling homemade cookies from our window.

Making it in a volatile business is like being in a potential storm every day. There's a small window of time to do something impactful, and we can't wait or we lose profits fast. The key is being nimble. Quick actions can be the very thing that keeps the business afloat. Other times it might actually bring you treasures of "wins"—like our now improved homemade doughnut mix. In this game, we have to be ready with as many preparations as possible—a steady team, good training, strategic menu items, a strong story, fun experiences—but we're also ready to react if things turn for the worse, demanding quick moves.

FIGHT THROUGH

There are enough difficulties to overcome in the restaurant business that your mindset matters a lot. We've barreled over the bumpy roads of a recession and a global pandemic, laying off every team member but one—including ourselves. We've fought harsh reviews, skepticism on new concepts, and periods of high turnover. In 2023, a street fight led to a shooting inside Growlers Pourhouse—two bullets were fired inside our doors. Jeff and all three of our children were there that night.

Maintaining a level, positive mindset even amid the shadows of huge problems shrinks them to a more manageable size. Then you get in there and fight your battles. But persistence through life sometimes requires more of you personally than you ever thought imaginable.

We opened Haberdish and Reigning Doughnuts in back-to-back years, 2016 and 2017. NoDa continued to grow. More people moved in, and the light-rail opened up, connecting our restaurants to a broad public transportation system. The neighborhood was becoming a destination, especially for weekend visits. At the time, we had our most ambitious project yet on the horizon in a church space with over eight thousand square feet, two separate buildings, and a garden area—Supperland. Our world was shiny and delicious with healthy babies, a growing team, and businesses with growth trends over 25 percent a year. But a key piece to all of it was missing, because I, myself, was heading down a spiral in the opposite direction.

Not yet forty years old, with three children and four successful restaurants, my body and my mind were beginning to fail me. Like tiny cracks just beginning to splinter apart, the problem was widening and worsening, eager to unearth a side of me I had never known. It started simply, with an expected sort of ailment, so unextraordinary it easily masked a much deeper problem.

As a former collegiate basketball player, I chalked my joint pain up to college athletics. Anyone who had played as much basketball as I did on wood floors, asphalt, and cement could expect joint pain later in life. But my pain was worsening—fast. It started with my hip. Then the aching migrated to my left knee and my left foot. My doctor put me in a boot off and on for years for intense plantar fasciitis. Cortisone pumped into my foot did nothing, and platelet-rich plasma injections in my foot and hip followed with no improvement. Physical therapy plateaued my pain, but at least I wasn't worsening. I cut out running because my gait had become hobble-like. Eventually I stopped walking for exercise too.

Other physical problems crept up, like ulceration. I went to a specialist an hour away in Winston-Salem to find out why I had fifteen actively painful ulcers all over my body. They tested me for some rare autoimmune diseases. I had nothing the doctor could diagnose.

Soon it wasn't just about physical pain. I couldn't define why, but I felt sad. Sometimes I'd be sitting at Crêpe Cellar, having dinner with Jeff and the kids, and my eyes would pan around the beautifully candlelit room. Instead of seeing the loveliness, all I felt was a looming sadness. Good things that used to brighten my day—like a fun article about our restaurants—just triggered loneliness. Music sent me toward melancholy. Thoughts of the children made me fearful for their health and safety instead of appreciative of the joy and gratitude that we were all alive together. I wanted to hide from the sadness, but there was nowhere to go. It was right with me every day.

Jeff and I started struggling. From my vantage point, he couldn't get anything right. He frustrated me and angered me, instead of inspiring me like he once had. Time passed and I devolved. The sadness became depression, then anxiety, then worse.

My first panic attack happened on Easter Sunday 2018. I was sitting in my backyard at our patio table with friends. Jeff had made duck tacos and fresh blue corn tortillas with gorgeously colorful accoutrements—pickled onions, roasted corn, and homemade salsa. As I looked at all the beauty surrounding me, I suddenly had to excuse myself. "I'll be back in a minute."

I hurried up to my room and sat on my bed. I leaned to my side and gently rocked. Tears streamed down my face, my heart raced, a chill spread through my body. Then a flash, like a jolt, shot through me like a wave. *What is happening to me?* After slow-moving minutes, my body calmed as my heart rate dropped, and I rolled off the side of the bed to sit up.

I caught my eyes in the long mirror on the wall. *What the hell was that?* I went into the bathroom and took some deep breaths. *I hope that never happens again. Ever.* I wasn't fully recovered, but a sudden embarrassment that I had taken too long inside came over me. *I should get back out there.* I shook out my hands and walked back downstairs to the kitchen, calmer than I had been but overcome that whatever that was would happen again. Our dinner party continued out the back door, separated from me by a glass door—and the foggy confusion in my mind. To all of them, time had passed normally, and nothing unusual had filled the last ten minutes but laughter and spooning seconds. Whatever had happened was apparently all in my mind.

I walked toward the table and smiled, wiggling my legs over the bench to sit down. The colors of the napkins and the bowls with bright salsas— all of it was still there. Vivid yellow circular placemats peeked from under blue bowls and small sheet pans. Warm homemade tortillas stayed hidden under a cloth napkin. People were smiling like normal, and I guess nothing had happened—to them. I ate slower that night, searching for clues, trying to understand why everyone else seemed so happy while, within my mind, life was darkness.

A single panic attack sucks. I began having these attacks every day and without warning. They were relentless. Most nights I shuttered myself in my room or bathroom to be alone so I didn't have to show my face in the worst of it. If this was what life was going to feel like, I no longer wanted to be here. My mind battled itself, certain that there'd be less suffering on earth if I just departed. Suicidal thoughts grew and fought to dominate my mind.

I stayed home as much as I could. If we ventured out, my mind flickered from one worry to the next—about my children dying or being sick, about my own death, about having to be here on earth and not wanting to be. Sometimes I excused myself to be alone and bring my heart rate down, to hold my dark thoughts back by breathing and reciting the 23rd Psalm on repeat. But there was no way out. There was nothing here for me to live for anymore.

Daytime brought glimmers of sanity, and in those moments, *none of it made sense*. I was ridden with anxiety and panic, but my life was abundant with "goodness." My kids were healthy. My husband was kind, loyal, and loving. Our businesses were thriving. My parents were healthy. I had a good job—a fun job—and because Jeff always handled the accounting, taxes, hiring/firing, and financials, a job with few stressors too.

It didn't make sense.

Still, these feelings haunted me. I was stuck, and the anxiety made me unable to handle my day-to-day life. One afternoon, a wave of panic rushed over me while talking to a guest at a table. I quickly left their side, grabbed my things, and went out to my car—an embarrassingly abrupt departure. Another weekend, when Jeff was going out of town, he wouldn't leave me with the children. I was thirty-nine, and no longer a trusted partner or parent. My twin sister came to help. Little did I know, I was still on my way downward.

High anxiety—which I had never battled before in my life—was an arduous road, and regular panic attacks made it even worse. I had no idea what I'd get any day of the week; all I could do was hope every day that it wasn't going to be a really bad day. I wasn't in a place to be creative or lead our team. Most days, I fought to move from one part of the day to the next. Morning. Afternoon. Evening. Night. Repeat. Evenings and nights were the hardest: pinging, zinging thoughts that I'd be better off dead and blustering, uncontrollable feelings that I didn't want to see my kids get older because there was nothing good to look forward to.

Depression and anxiety are hard to explain to anyone who hasn't lived it. People say things like "Just stop feeling that way" or "You have so much going for you" or "How could you be unhappy when there's so much good in the world?" or "You're just not being grateful for what you have." I understood all of that logically. It all made sense. But it wasn't my reality.

I was prescribed medication. Even though my doctor said it would stop a panic attack in about five minutes, I couldn't bring myself to take it. Looking back, I'm not entirely sure why I couldn't take the medicine. Maybe because I grew up in a household that kind of shunned medicine. But more than anything, I think it was because I didn't want to rely on something outside of myself to be well. I started therapy, and I went religiously. I had a hotline number, too, and sometimes I would just cling to my phone in the worst of it, thinking that maybe this time I would call, and that person, that stranger on the other end of the line, would make it all just go away. But usually, grasping my phone just ended up with me begging my doctor's office for an appointment.

My depression had a unique effect on me—I started baking like a madwoman. I didn't understand this staunch craving for sweets until months later, so I just went with it. I made chocolate chip cookie cakes with my grandmother Malu Audrey's recipe. I'd decorate the cookie cake with icing, piped beautifully with my children's names or sporting large round-petaled flowers over the surface. I learned to make pie—glorious, fruity, rich pie. I made pies on repeat: peach, blueberry, cherry. And then again. I wove my homemade pie crust over the top and cut out etched leaves to place over the weave. I ate most of them myself, unknowingly allowing those treats to prop my dangerously swinging mood with regular injections of quick carbohydrates.

The religious household I grew up in had me trained to pray—for help, for guidance, for anything—and I prayed a lot. *Rescue me. Help me find answers. Lead me to something that can make me well again.* Answers were far away. I had built up an incredible repertoire of calming techniques with my therapist, and they helped when my anxiety was mild, but the panic attacks were too big to quell. Their force came with ease and power, flooding over any of my paltry efforts to calm my mind.

I had been battling daily panic attacks for months with no change. Then one night in August of 2018, I shot out of bed at 2 a.m. with a strange, unprompted thought. *Could this be about bugs? Bacteria?* Thoughts of animal diseases like rabies weirdly floated into my mind. After all, why would a human battle with taking their own life if there isn't something else driving that? I grabbed my phone, desperate to find new answers.

The unusual thought sent me down a rabbit hole of research, uncovering insights about the gut microbiome, inflammation, sugar intolerances, food sensitivities, and autoimmune reactions. Then it hit me: My identical twin sister had been diagnosed with type 1 diabetes at the age of thirty-one.

What if I wasn't crazy?

What if I was reacting to what I was eating?

With some more research and online health professional advice, I rid my diet of any of the most likely triggers for physical and mental food reactions. I was hoping to get answers about whatever was going on inside of me, and then find a way to claw myself out.

I committed to a three-month elimination diet to remove grains, gluten, dairy, sugar, nightshades (a plant family including tomatoes, potatoes, goji berries, eggplant, peppers, and more), soy, nuts, seeds (including chocolate and coffee), and even fruit and starchier vegetables too. There were certain types of vegetables I was advised to avoid with my symptoms, so I kept out the FODMAPs family of vegetables, which includes brussels sprouts, onions, garlic, cabbage, and cauliflower. Within a week, I discovered that I got itchy every time I ate carrots and celery, so I took those out too. I was down to very few foods. For what ended up being four months, day after day, I ate some mixture of okra, zucchini, yellow squash, ground turkey, shrimp, cucumber, grass-fed beef, avocado, coconut, lettuce, and some mushrooms. For flavors, I stuck to salt, olive oil, apple cider vinegar, lemon, and lime.

I cooked in bulk at home, eating out of glass storage containers for most meals. When we traveled, I brought homemade coconut chips and whole avocados to tide me over. When eating out at any restaurant, I asked for simply grilled meats, chicken, or seafood, usually over a bed of lettuce with olive oil and vinegar. Jeff and I began seeking steakhouses that did plain grilling of proteins and vegetables because they could easily modify to my food preferences. Steakhouses made me feel normal again—like I could almost eat like other people, like I was healing, and like I had hope to be normal again someday.

The impact of my diet shift was earth-shattering. That first week I changed my diet was the last week I had a panic attack. While it was an unconventional answer, I knew what I had to do. I could again hope to live a bold, strong, empowered life. What I intended to be a three-month elimination diet continues to be the base of my primary diet today, many years later. Once I started paying attention, I connected food to all the other symptoms I had too.

The mental illness was the most challenging and "painful" of my symptoms, but over the years, I've suffered from so many different health issues. With dots connected, my reactions to food have included: anxiety, depression, and panic attacks (the worst of my symptoms); ulceration; numbness in my arms, fingers, or areas of my face; knife-like tingling on my back;

constipation; bumpy nails; geographic tongue (splotches on the tongue); vision changes; C-shaped floaters in my eyes; debilitating joint pain; sleeplessness; severe bloating; throat itchiness; dry eye; dry mouth; grinding teeth; vivid, hallucination-like nightmares; gout in my toe; heart palpitations; headaches; dizziness; uncontrollable finger twitching; and calcification of my upper back to the point that I couldn't get out of bed on my own.

Getting back to "normal" after going through this radical health discovery changed my every day going forward—and it looks different now than I imagined. While I keep my base diet tight, over the last few years, I've been able to add some ingredients in limited quantities.

It took me years of food journaling, but I came away with tremendous insights on how food makes me feel and how I can craft a strong mental state through my diet. What I learned through research and experimentation: I have a lot of food sensitivities, some of which impact my mental health through the gut-brain connection. I now eat gluten-free and grain-free, and I limit a lot of other foods to very small quantities—nuts, soy, sugars of any kind, dairy, seeds, nightshade vegetables, new world vegetables (like butternut or spaghetti squash), and carbs in general. I hope to someday gain the confidence to add more foods back to my diet even in small doses. I stay open to change. By necessity, I came to understand something attributed to Aristotle from a couple thousand years ago: "Through discipline comes freedom."

I've heard a part of us must die in order to truly live. We must let go of what we were to become a new, higher version of ourselves. Through the discipline I bring each day, I witness the best me available right now. That process of daily mindfulness allows for my ongoing evolution, long after the excruciating process of having my eyes unveiled.

My radical change in diet saved my life physically and mentally. I understand that my mental illness stemmed from my gut health—and so I'm not afraid of it coming back. I've wrestled myself free from debilitating panic attacks. And equally powerful, my hour-by-hour life is no longer flooded with anxiousness. I feel bold, confident, self-assured, and like this whole beautiful game of life is here as a gift. I've garnered trust in the

Universe and in myself to ask, believe, and find answers in any difficulty. I have faced the most difficult enemy one can—the self. Yet, I befriended her and rose.

That rising only emboldened me, and it came at the perfect time, because Jeff and I had an incredibly large project to start up: Supperland. We dreamed it would be special for Charlotte, and maybe, just maybe, break out beyond our locale and receive broader acclaim. Our passion, ideas, creativity, and work all aimed high, and now I had the clarity of mind and abounding confidence to take it on.

Of course, now I had all these food sensitivities as a restaurant owner. But it turned out that this ironic and demanding food challenge would be a key ingredient in our ability to create bolder, more adaptable, more inclusive dining experiences for our guests—a critical X factor that helped push us to the next level.

SERVING SPOON: All those difficulties and challenges are there to help you become the person you dream of being, and they'll help carve your business into a stronger entity too. Lean into the challenge, lean into the imperfections—they're there to help.

Six

TEAMWORK

The right ingredients make the dish.

On one busy block in NoDa, we were operating four concepts, with about 130 teammates coming and going, prepping food, taking back-alley cigarette breaks, and sharing anything like eggs or bananas or the meat smoker stacked in the kitchen of Haberdish. Some people took shifts at multiple places; others coupled up together as partners or room-mates. The trash and recycling and composting from all four places poured into the same dumpsters, and beer kegs piled up in a walled area between the concepts. We were woven tightly together.

From the outside, the businesses appeared to be unique—and to guests, they were. The menus were all different at Ever Andalo, Haberdish, Growlers Pourhouse, and Reigning Doughnuts. Each had a different story, different character elements, and each evoked different feelings for patrons. But behind the scenes was an integrated back-of-house system of teamwork, imperfect but high-functioning, putting out delicious food and top-notch service for each of the concepts. The intricate inner workings of these four restaurants serving homemade dishes to thousands of people every week, succeeding within the constraints of low margins and small spaces, felt like some sort of divine miracle.

Achieving that miracle, though, required over a decade of persisting in a continuously evolving business. Our initial eleven tables led to another concept and then another and another. Each led to new jobs, to creating an inspiring place to work, to getting higher-level experts on our team, to embracing more ambitious projects, and getting better at what we do—all of us, together.

A DANCE

Jeff's and my early days in the restaurant business were not easy. We had our first baby, Isabella, just a few months after opening. Because I had taken a job when I was already four months pregnant, the company gave me only six weeks of maternity leave, unpaid. As a new and breastfeeding mom, I found myself strapped twice a day t.;o an electrical outlet. My employers didn't give me a specific place to pump, so I moved from a bathroom to an office to a storage closet to a locker room over the course of five months. As the first woman to have a child at that company, I was forging a new path, and it wasn't pretty.

In hindsight, I should have fought for more—I might have smoothed the road for future young moms—but I was desperate to keep my job. I was barely pulling a B-minus grade across life: stepping away from work to pump, then stepping away from my brand-new baby to get a paycheck. The guilt was heavy, and on both ends. Even though I was giving all I had, I still felt like I wasn't enough at any of the important things.

On the north side of town, Jeff was at Crêpe Cellar during the mornings, often with Isabella strapped to his chest. For a few hours in the middle of the afternoon, our nanny, Nancy, kept the baby at home until I could get there for the evening pass-off. Jeff would often stop home at the end of my workday to see me before he left to manage a shift at the restaurant. Our arrangement, like a dance every day, worked for us because it had to work.

Like any married couple, over the years, Jeff and I have had ups and downs. We've had near-sleepless nights with babies, passing off diaper changings, rockings, and feedings. We tag-teamed the intense middle-grade activities and navigated schoolwork, peer groups, technology, and bedtimes. We have dozens of LLCs together, some for real estate, some restaurants, some restaurant support. Our 1904 house always needs fixing. Our parents are aging. A host of teammates rely on us to care for them. We've stood beside each other through failures and stayed up late to celebrate successes. Our journey took us around the world and through the confusion of getting back on our feet. We are, in tandem, building a vision for our growing company. Our connections run deep, and while not always shiny and perfect, they're grounded in love.

Our strong partnership crosses over to help our business operations in immeasurable ways. For one, our company doesn't have a lot of red tape. We have some, and it's necessary—otherwise it would be a free-for-all with every team member enacting new ways of doing things at every whim. But for Jeff and me, if we mutually feel strongly about something, we just do it. While we consider the counsel of leaders on our team, we don't have to seek approval to buy a 1915 church building, rebrand a concept, start a new service, or anything else that might be out of the ordinary in typical business operations.

We also complement each other. Jeff is logical and mathematical, and I'm more on the whimsical side. At the same time, though, I tend to be grounded in my responsibilities, whereas he is ready for a fun time all the time. Our strengths and ways of doing things balance each other. When we have a new restaurant to name, I'll jot down pages and pages of ideas— many of them straight from the clouds. They're weird and they're wacky. But he'll look them over and see the ones that fit. The ones he gravitates toward tend to have a balance of creativity and groundedness. Finding this balance requires humility on both our parts, an awareness that we cannot get attached to anything unless it receives the stamp from the other.

We build from our shared decades of lived experience. When we're conceptualizing a new restaurant, this is especially helpful. I recount memories that have inherent mutual meaning to both of us. I say to him, "Remember in Grenada when the Flamenco dancers came and swung around the room?" Or "Remember when we were in the cellar of the Pommery in Reims, and the artwork that led us through the tunnels?" Or "Remember the fluffy fabric on the bar stools at that restaurant in Chicago?" Countless stories serve as starting points for our creative pursuits.

Having a precise direction is critical for our buildouts, and sometimes there are moments of "Oh! I thought you meant you wanted the full wall to be emerald green" or "Oh! I was envisioning something more gothic and less modern." We banter, we share pictures, we make our cases. Then we move forward again, narrowing in on the same page.

Last, we dream together. Sometimes at night, Jeff and I turn the lights off in our family room and sit quietly, with just a candle flickering. Sometimes we go for long walks and chatter away about new ideas. Sometimes we visit one of our restaurants to feel and ponder what else it needs. Sometimes we visit new spaces, even when we're not actively seeking a project. It keeps our minds open and geared up for what might be next.

Dreaming and imagining have been integral to our restaurant group's growth. I happen to be one who believes our authentic thoughts direct what happens in our physical world. But whether or not one subscribes to such theories, it seems clear that simply having a vision helps us make decisions that get us closer to our goals. It's forward thinking that helps us weigh what projects to take, what to seek out, and how to grow ourselves and our team. Without the guidance of our dreams, we'd travel as the wind blows and arrive anywhere it might take us. With concerted thought and direction, together with trust in one another, we overcome the notion of happenstance and gain greater control over our destination.

With a growing team of about three hundred right now, the dance isn't just between Jeff and me anymore. We have a group of people who overwhelmingly care about providing top-notch hospitality (and I don't mean perfect hospitality because we do have human beings working with us). Some of this "care" is selected for in the hiring process, and we've been lucky to attract some pretty amazing people. They show up every day and give their best. But that's not *everyone* on the team.

To enhance teamwork in service among the whole front of house staff, Jeff and I have adopted a specific tipping method. We like to use a pooled tip system—a system where tips are pooled together and divvied up at the end of the night. For our organization, it has done nothing but help engender teamwork where the whole front-of-house acts together to give their best service.

We first implemented tip pooling when we opened Haberdish in late 2016, and over the years, we've lost a number of servers who do not like sharing tips. They liked to take their own tips from their own tables and more or less run their own sales program to get the highest tickets and highest tips. But that doesn't always ensure we're taking the best care of our guests. We stick with a pooled tip system now because it gives our guests better service and creates a stronger team mentality on the floor.

It's fun to watch a tip-pool restaurant. A server from one table will fill the water glasses of another's. One server whispers to another that they need help, and others will pitch in. Server A takes the tray from Server B to bus plates quickly so they can ring up the bill and flip the table sooner. A napkin on a table gets folded by someone even though it's not "their" table, just because it will be better service for the guest. Bonds develop between servers who help one another get through a busy shift.

The tip pool has downsides, of course. As in any group, a few people don't pull their weight. Occasionally it's because they're lazy. Other times they're new and they haven't figured out how to make "upsells" at the table like a veteran server—things like encouraging guests to add a refreshing intermezzo to their meal or suggesting the addition of an order of blackened onions to elevate any steak cut at their Supperland feast. Some servers are just not as intense or driven as others. But as long as the restaurants remain busy, the tip pool has worked in our favor. Jeff and I eat out a lot, at restaurants all over the country, and we're always blown away by the level of service our staff achieves.

The number of people in very different roles makes this business tricky to keep running smoothly. We rely heavily on one another and give and take every day—each one of us attempting to dance to the beat, not step on toes, get the jobs done, and orchestrate a lovely dining experience.

TRUST IN THE TEAM

As Jeff and I seek greater growth for our business, we rely exponentially on our team to step up and handle tasks both big and small. Letting others do their work requires tremendous trust. Jeff and I create the direction of a concept—the restaurant story, the design, the layout—but then our job shifts. Without our team of professionals across the kitchen, bar, and front of house, we wouldn't be able to put forth what we have in our minds. Our teammates are integral to our one-of-a-kind dining establishments. Some develop training processes, some innovate menu items, some hire more teammates, and some make sure everyone gets paid. And our talented team couldn't bring the vision to life without our trust in them.

Social media has long been my jam. I was good at creating custom content and personal content for our restaurants on social media, but eventually, hiring someone to do the job was necessary so I could grow. It might seem like a small adjustment, but the decision had huge implications for the direction of our company. Trusting someone else with social media left me free to create new services, try new marketing efforts, do speaking engagements, write, find new spaces, and open up potential new growth directions. My letting go gave the team more ownership in the job, plus I had more time to carve out for those big dreams.

Delegating responsibilities is the only way Jeff and I don't get eaten alive by our restaurants. Don't get me wrong, there is a lot of oversight to make strategic changes. If a dish isn't right in a tasting, we make it again, and again, and again. Then we pull together the general manager, chefs, and prep cooks to make sure everyone understands the quality specifications of that item. Then the execution of the new plan falls on the team.

Because we have a passionate, capable team managing and running service each day, this leaves Jeff and me free to forge ahead into larger business development initiatives like looking for new spaces, running numbers on new service opportunities, or crafting events or interesting ways of bringing people through our doors. We can also focus on big-picture improvements to enhance our margins, raise our quality, add better service points, and streamline strategic operations. Our restaurant group takes on the most ambitious projects in the city because we've got the best talent around. And our teammates get new responsibilities and growth experiences, as well as higher-paying job opportunities, with our focus on growth.

Entrepreneurs are often fantastic at starting with their heads in the clouds, but once a business is launched, drifting into the clouds is not only permissible, it may be exactly what's needed to take a venture to another level. Someone needs to be at the helm of any business, and that person has a responsibility to look up and see where the ship is headed. Dreaming requires trusting in the efforts of those around you.

In the current restaurant business climate, there are many nuances to expertise, and it is difficult to have knowledge that crosses every element of the experience. From wine to liquor to local products to cooking techniques to sourcing unique seasonal produce, we rely on the breadth and depth of our team's expertise to maintain high standards.

Michael Klinger, a level-three sommelier, brought an entirely new degree of wine knowledge to our team. His influence has brought on rosé garden parties, wine dinners, tastings, educational opportunities for our staff, wine lists hundreds of labels long, and guest inquiries for select wine dinners. Colleen Hughes's ongoing cocktail expertise is shared across each of our places as she guides the drink menus and training for our bartenders. Our Supperland pastry chef, Savannah Foltz, shares her knowledge of pastry, breads, and sweets so our whole team stays fresh and seasonal, and we continually train newer pastry team members. Top-level managers like Moriah Glenn and Jon Rosenberg hold the whole pulsing restaurant together—front and back of house. It's a ton of different challenges that they face each day, from building maintenance to sourcing to staffing issues. Their ability to juggle and keep the ship afloat is awe-inspiring.

Our right-hand woman, Lindsey Robbins, is there for everything. She keeps accounting straight, she manages company-wide benefits, she steps in with larger HR problems, and she designs menus, hitting deadlines for all our special events. We cannot operate without her. We have two maintenance guys, Bryce and Jason, for woodworking, building tables, painting, general fix-up, light bulb switch-outs, chair and table maintenance, and whatever might happen within our walls with hundreds of people walking in and out every day. They keep the places in good physical shape. Our marketing and social media guru, Allie Papajohn, communicates with media; gets the word out for events, specials, and new items; and she keeps all websites, menus, and hours up to date. She shows the behind-the-scenes of our kitchens and tastings and makes sure we have the ever-important full dining rooms.

With a team of experts that meets and maintains high standards, we set both our business and ourselves up to win. Of course, this is easier to execute with a steady base of teammates who have acclimated to or helped build our cultural expectations. But even as turnover inevitably happens and people leave our restaurant family, the business culture not only remains intact but it can continue to thrive.

WORK FOR THEIR TRUST

A big part of the reason our company has seen strong growth is because of the trust we have in our team. But before that, Jeff and I had to first earn the trust of our teammates. One of the most impactful ways we've done that is through mindful pay structure.

In 2019, we did a scary, bold thing with hourly pay. We brought our whole team up to a living wage—a calculation that suggests what an individual needs to earn in order to actually live in a given area. This was a large financial endeavor that impacted all our restaurants. At the time, the living wage for our area was $14.37 per hour, while the minimum wage for North Carolina was a slight $7 per hour. No one on our team was earning $7 per hour, but we did have dishwashers or cleaning crew as low as $11 per hour.

One of the most challenging aspects of this financial move was that it wasn't just our lowest-paid teammates who got a raise. Every teammate who worked in the kitchen got at least a $2-per-hour raise to keep respective pay in line with responsibilities and tasks. A prep cook usually gets paid about a dollar an hour more than a dishwasher, and a line cook gets paid about a dollar an hour more than a prep cook. In many cases, this was a double-digit percent raise for individuals, and in the first year alone, the cost of this change for the whole company was about $20,000. Of course, once we committed to that pay raise, it hit the balance sheet each year. Plus, as Charlotte continues to grow exponentially, so does the living wage. In 2023, we reassessed our pay levels and brought the base staff wage to $16.83 an hour to maintain a living wage for our teammates.

Across our businesses, to cover wages, we find small gaps where we can justifiably increase a price or offer higher-end items to increase revenue. Steak toppers like our crab with miso butter can add an extra $18 to a table. Adding a pull-apart pork belly entrée option to our dinner menu at Haberdish helped increase the average check size. Sometimes Jeff and I take a personal hit. We've also bumped up our expectations for labor operating expenses from about 35 percent to closer to 40 percent.

There is subjectivity in the calculation of a living wage, with nuance, timing, and disparities from one zip code to the next. But because we keep an eye on it and make changes with the broader economy, our employees know that we want to improve their quality of life. The individuals on our team are in a better place income-wise than restaurant workers have been throughout history, with huge jumps in the last handful of years. We want our teammates to see the beautiful things in life, but it's hard to dream if you don't have enough money to get by. Dreaming is a luxury.

Our commitment to raise pay as a company has been a large driver in our retaining a strong and inspired team, as has our commitment toward continuous learning for individuals. But beyond this, we have a few unusual approaches to staffing, team building, and management that have allowed us to thrive.

First, we hold an "everyone is welcome" mentality. We value diversity. In shift meetings, people of all races, ages, religions, genders, and sexual orientations come together to move the business forward. One of my favorite moments every year is to take a team photo at our annual Friendsgiving. I'll look at that photo throughout the year, zooming in on people's faces and all the unique features, colors, and attire. There's someone with purple hair, another with goth makeup, another fully tattooed, another with face piercings, another wearing all leather, another in gigantic platform shoes with poking metal protrusions, another with hardly anything on at all. To me, it is the most beautiful rainbow of people—each one so different from the next and each one as humanly valuable as the next too. I simply love them, and I love their differences. It brings me joy. We have a beautiful patchwork of people, and we all support one another and keep the ship moving forward, even if imperfectly.

Our system is not flawless. We are all real people, and sometimes real people are broken—whether because of personal disappointments, difficult upbringings, drug and alcohol use, mental illness, and general coming-of-age challenges with a young staff. But I sincerely dream that our restaurant group will continue to be an impetus for individuals to embrace new ideas, honor people, and open minds and hearts to further humanity in love.

Another mentality that has positively impacted our labor pool is for Jeff and me to butt out and not micromanage our team. We are meticulous, thoughtful, and detail-oriented in creating a concept. But when it's time to let go, we step back and allow managers, shift leads, servers, bartenders, and chefs to lead the way. We move into a leadership/guidance role. It doesn't take much time before our team is more well-versed in the happenings of a restaurant than we are. They know what positions need to be filled, who's causing issues in the kitchen, who did a "no call, no show," and what items are upselling really well. They are immersed in the restaurant, so their opinions are valuable and respected. We keep guide rails up, but our managers are running the daily show.

Next, Jeff and I focus on a growth pipeline. Pipelines mean opportunity for the company and all the people working for our company. We pave the road ahead for new, unique restaurant opportunities, and our teammates rise into new skill sets and responsibilities. It's seeing possibility in a run-down window to sell hot doughnuts. It's envisioning the rehabilitation of an unsightly building. It's keeping our eyes open for cracked doors that could lead to something bigger. We started with about twenty employees; we are now around three hundred. Because of our ongoing growth, we've attracted individuals who are passionate about a career in hospitality and eager for opportunities to rise.

I don't have a lot of time to spend with every individual on our team. I won't get to know many of them well—where they come from, what their home life is like, what their darkest moments have been, and what their hopes and dreams are. Some of them, I'll never even know their names. The restaurant business is fluid, so many people who have been dear to us have gone away to follow their own dreams, their own path—and I expect them to. We have to be fluid and flexible and unfettered. I try not to get attached, but the thing is, I still do. I've cried when someone decided to leave us in what feels to me like a time too soon. I've sobbed when someone on our team hit a roadblock—a sickness, a death in the family, a divorce, or a breakup. They're not my problems, but I wish life could be easier for everyone.

Teammates come and go. Our restaurants serve as a holding spot, a safe haven, an island in the middle of a wide sea. Often people come to work in this industry while they're busy concocting other plans. They hang for a while, get money to pay bills, and see if they can hack it—as an actor, an artist, in real estate, or as a musician. It's the nature of this business. We often welcome teammates back, understanding that it may not be a jubilant moment for that person who has returned. It might feel like a step backward for them. They may have fallen when they tried something new, or gotten rejected by a job, or had their heart broken.

Sometimes, even with hard work and belief, plans don't turn out the way we hope.

So, when I say, "Welcome back," I say it with a love that's intermixed with sobered feelings. Familiar faces bring me joy—that they felt safe to return and confident that we would find a spot for them. But I am mindful that it's not always the story they hoped for. We're here as a safe, trusted place to return should they need it down the road.

SHOW UP

Sometimes in this business, we haven't known how to help teammates. Sometimes we walk a line of what's good and what's bad, and I'm not the best fit to judge that decision. Sometimes we follow our heart and hope we're doing the right thing—but we don't always *know* we're doing the right thing.

Late one night, after a swell of tension and mockery, one of our bar managers punched a mouthy guest straight across the jaw after receiving a punch in the head from behind. We put the manager on probation, but after we came to understand more details, we hired him back to our team. I don't know if it was the right thing to do, but once you are working alongside people, they become part of your team. You trust their story.

Love isn't always pristine. It isn't always crystal clear. But for us, it has been about showing up in whatever you're wearing to help whomever needs help and with whatever resources you can drum up in that specific instance.

Chef Ruth and our bar manager, Hannah, had been dating for years, and they spontaneously decided to do a courthouse wedding—with no actual reservation time for an appointment. They were turned away from the courthouse. Still determined to get married on that specific day— February 22, 2022—our team jumped into action. Growlers Pourhouse would be the venue. With its worn brick walls, stained cement floor, and large rectangular windows showcasing Thirty-Fifth Street, it had enough space to mock up an aisle with friends lining the room. Our general manager from Haberdish, just three doors down, happened to be ordained, so she was called in to conduct the ceremony. The kitchen sent out a handful of appetizers for the guests.

At the far end of the restaurant, by the bathroom hallway, Jeff took his position—wearing a light-yellow, stained T-shirt inappropriate for any wedding but this impromptu one. He took the arms of both Ruth and Hannah, and they walked through the center of the restaurant, heading toward the front door and the busy sidewalk of North Davidson Street. Just short of the ten-top table up front, the trio stopped. Jeff leaned right and kissed Hannah on the forehead. He leaned left and kissed Ruth on the forehead. Then he stepped away.

In Harry Potter thematics, the ceremony continued, and the two women wedded that night. Cortney, our Haberdish manager and wedding officiant, spoke to the room: "Dumbledore said, 'Happiness can be found even in the darkest of times if one only remembers to turn on the light.' JK Rowling. Be each other's light, and when life brings you darkness, look to each other and find happiness there." She continued, "In front of your friends and these bar patrons, it is my pleasure to pronounce you, by the power vested in me by the Ministry of Magic, wives and partners for life."

Jeff's and my involvement in our teammates' lives is varied. We've hosted a quinceañera celebration for a staff member's daughter, bailed an employee out of jail, and attended the funeral and celebration of life of another. We've written letters to landlords to help staff find accommodations. We've been to art shows and baby showers and birthdays. Some of us are raising kids at the same time. I've sat bedside of a teammate's mother at the hospital, attempting to translate the doctor's words with my broken understanding of Spanish. We created an art studio in our garage for a teammate to take steps forward with his passion. We conducted fundraisers and matching programs to get someone out of a "hole." We've purchased paintings, paid down payments for cars, and created positions to keep a team member on staff.

These are small stories of love from my little window of the restaurant world. But there are countless stories of people showing up for one another throughout our restaurant group. Showing up comes in many forms, but the reason we show up is *love*. And love only ever brings about more love. That foundation is the beginning of building a beautiful, impactful team.

While we each get a different piece of our business's pie, my hope is that as the pie grows, everyone may continue to reap more from what they do. I hope I do my part in growing that pie so that everyone gets more. Each person on our team is a thread that holds the whole organization together, and I'm in awe of it. I hope they each feel they are a part of something bigger than themselves and that they'll be inspired to follow their own dreams too. Mostly, I just wish them love. Love has looked like a lot of things to us over the years—ever evolving, ever shifting—but ever present.

TRUST AGAIN

One night, the cash bag at Crêpe Cellar, stuffed with more than $4,000, went missing. With only three potential culprits, Jeff and I scoured the video footage, retraced our steps from the afternoon leading into the evening, and thought through pertinent conversations. One potential thief was a young man, a server with us for a handful of years. The two others were women who had been on our team over ten years. They had children and families. The likelihood of any one of them stealing the bag was low. There was nothing outright incriminating in the footage, but through a process of elimination, it became clear that our friend and server—let's call him "Decker"—had taken the bag.

It's not easy to call out someone for stealing, especially when they've become dear to you. Decker had worked with us for over five years. He was a big part of everyday service, and we trusted him. After the bag was stolen, Jeff asked him to meet up at one of our restaurants in the middle of the day. One of our chefs served as a silent witness. Decker walked up to where Jeff was sitting. Jeff leaned forward. "Bring back the cash bag, and I will not press charges."

Decker was caught off guard. He didn't think we'd find out. He had planned on continuing with work as usual.

Within thirty minutes the bag was returned with every cent inside of it. Decker apologized and asserted that he had not stolen anything before from the company.

The money was deposited, and our friend left the team that day. We didn't press charges. We could have and perhaps should have. It was an easy case, and he probably needed to learn a lesson. But Jeff and I are not here to make life difficult for anyone. A lot of people—especially broken people— need a second chance. To act with the utmost love, we must forgive. Rather than chasing after criminal behavior, we just let it go.

For our own benefit, it's not only about forgiveness, it's also about trusting again. This wasn't the only time we've had money stolen from us by a coworker, but to lead greatly, we cannot get stuck in the anger, frustration, or condemnation of others. We move forward with our mindset defaulted on trust in both the world and in our growing number of teammates.

SERVING SPOON: Are you acting with full trust in your team, allowing them to do their part, to rise, to contribute, to grow? Even though it's scary to trust, this is a key foundation on which to grow.

Seven

MANAGE RISK

Tempered eggs don't scramble.

With 3–5 percent margins on average and most restaurants failing early in their lifetimes, managing risk is imperative for the short- and long-term. We go to great lengths to keep our business in check with both larger strategic decisions and daily processes. All the fun and beauty of dining out can only come about because of the diligence and unglamorous behind-the-scenes actions of managing risk.

CHEAT CODES

There are hundreds of efforts we make to keep food costs in line as we operate, but one notable component is having some sort of cheat code— an inherent trait, or skill, or way of doing things that simply makes us operate better. For an athlete, a cheat code might be size, vertical jump, or uncanny peripheral vision; some trait sets the athlete apart and helps them compete better. Restaurants can be like this too. There are built-in elements of different restaurant concepts or processes that inherently make it easier to hit profitability numbers and grow.

At Supperland, the expectation that each dinner guest will spend about $100 is a huge cheat code for us. On the aggregate, when our diners walk in our door, they get close to hitting that mark. Supperland is, in large part, a celebration restaurant, so we welcome guests on a night when they're wanting and willing to spend more on something like our seafood tower. Servers hold that heavy tower from the chilly ice-filled bottom rising up with two tiers and packed with raw Blue Point oysters, U-8 shrimp (these are the big boys!), white fish ceviche, and lump crab. It's celebration food at its finest.

We have a different cheat code at Haberdish: incredible efficiencies in cooking up fried chicken. While we brine the chicken for nearly half a day in buttermilk, the cooking process is fast, which allows us to serve more guests in a timely manner, turn our tables more each night, and keep guests happy with food that arrives on time and hot at the table. Crispy, browned, fresh-fried chicken is our staple there, going out to nearly every party. Our primary entrée, the item we are most well-known for, sails us through successful service each shift.

At Ever Andalo, pasta happens to be a very high-margin item. Chefs mix up flour and water (and maybe egg, as in our cavatelli pasta dough)—but these are relatively inexpensive ingredients (except eggs at times!). The dough combines and gets kneaded out, and then it runs through our pasta maker. Long sheets of pasta get thinner and thinner until they're ready to be cut. Each long-noodle portion is weighed out and nestled in a nest, ready to be dropped into a boiling pot. After a quick one to two minutes, the pasta is ready for the saucepan where something like our Bucatini all'Amatriciana is tossed with guanciale and homemade San Marzano tomato sauce. A fresh grating of Pecorino Romano, then we top off the dish with a sprig of basil. Guests are willing to pay over $20 a plate because of the attention to detail. There is a lot of thoughtfulness in the simplicity of our pastas, but the ingredients themselves allow for a good margin item. Having some super profitable offerings like this in our menu mix helps us hit our overall food costs.

Another cheat code that our restaurant group has is our talent and drive toward creating new concepts. Jeff and I love to build out new restaurants. For a lot of people, this is stressful, scary, and they might worry they won't nail another concept. By following our hearts, we've keyed in on something we're pretty good at and something we love to do. Our team leans into that, and growth happens—another restaurant is created, and more opportunities arise.

Each time we open a restaurant, we take the same deliberate, step-by-step approach: Launch the concept, get it steadied, and look for another opportunity to rise into. Once we step aside, each place is set up with an incredible team of people who are passionate and care about the business's growth.

We've repeated this cycle over and over again:

> 2009: Crêpe Cellar opened with eleven tables
>
> 2010: Growlers Pourhouse opened
>
> 2013: Crêpe Cellar expanded to twenty tables
>
> 2016: Haberdish opened
>
> 2017: Reigning Doughnuts opened
>
> 2021: Supperland opened
>
> 2022: Crêpe Cellar closed and the location rebranded
>   as Ever Andalo
>
> 2025: Leluia Hall opened

Over the years, our timeline shows progress, and in the space between dates, we are acclimating to new business operations, teammates, requirements, and challenges. Without those pauses, we'd overburden our lives and risk unsteadying the whole system. Once the business is steadied, looking toward the next peak is possible. Starting over at each new concept is one of the most exciting parts of the cycle. We get to go on the journey again. We create all over again, with more people and bigger ideas and more experience. That joy cheat code is part of the reason we keep growing.

Besides Jeff and I loving to build out new restaurants, another cheat code our team has is Jeff's and my personal interconnectedness with all our restaurants. Our restaurants are totally intertwined into our lives—it's what we love to do, and it's a big part of our life purpose. That passion carries over into our personal life, where our time together is often spent nurturing and streamlining these places we've built.

On a morning walk together, the cool breeze reminded Jeff and me that it wasn't quite springtime. Pollen coated the cars with a light-yellow dusting, but the grass was a tiny bit crunchy from a cold night. We edged across South Boulevard into busy South End. Four doughnut shops operate within walking distance of our house, and we were on a recon mission to inform some strategic changes at Reigning Doughnuts.

From shop to shop, rows of colorful icings and sprinkles and jellies goggled at us from behind clear glass. Sprinkles in elegant golds, shimmering and round, and others like a rainbow had burst in the kitchen and sprayed every color imaginable over a tray of newly fried dough. Some featured tight dollops of cream, others a wistful dust of powdered sugar, and still others were adorned with intricate, feathery icing showing off killer piping skills.

All four shops priced their doughnuts higher than ours—by a lot. Our doughnuts are cake doughnuts. They don't need time to rise, nor are they filled. They're a pretty normal size, too—nothing gigantic. But our competitors' doughnuts were priced anywhere from $1 to $3 more *per piece* than our doughnuts. Our prices had risen moderately over the years, but that day, other offerings in the market made it clear to us that a price hike was warranted.

That bond between the business and the personal sets us up for regular changes, adjustments, and improvements to help our businesses thrive, like in the case of doughnut prices. That morning walk had a big impact over the course of a year. By raising the price of a single doughnut from $2.00 to $2.50, and assuming we sell 350 doughnuts each day, that's an additional $175/day, or $54,250 a year. You may sell fewer doughnuts due to the price increase, but you're still on the positive side unless there's a drop of over 20 percent in your sales. Little tweaks to a menu's pricing can have a huge ripple effect on a restaurant's bottom line—and we've always got our eyes open to making those little improvements.

We've dabbled outside our cheat codes to bring up sales—like selling T-shirts and hats at Haberdish or selling our custom plates at Supperland. We've found success in shifting margins upward by renting out our spaces for events. When a large group needs a space, they are often willing to pay a space rental fee or even do a "buyout" of the restaurant—something that can be very lucrative for a shift. Still, we don't count on these alternative one-off income streams to keep us afloat; for us, those built-in cheat codes are primary difference-makers over the long haul.

BEND THE UNFAVORABLE

On our track to manage risk, we have learned to let the unexpected, even the seemingly undesirable, work for us. This open, positive mindset has allowed our business to be nimble, capitalizing, creative, and differentiated. We look at a situation to see the opportunity, then we flip it to our advantage and create results that serve us. This is managing risk by creating more certainty and harnessing control back to your side.

There's a lot of potential risk in our world. About three hundred people work across our six locations, all of which are older properties. Three thousand dishes go out to guests every day. Produce arrives from farmers all over the Southeast, and ingredients make their way from around the world. Crops sometimes have a poor yield. Shipments get lost or damaged. Vacations happen. Injuries occur. Toilets clog. People get sick. Chairs break. Machinery malfunctions. Pandemics happen. Storms flood basements.

Sometimes the wrenches aren't negative, but stuff happens that interrupts our flow. People get married and leave. Staff get pregnant. Someone gets an offer for a higher paying job. You name it, we've seen it, and it's probably impacted our business in some way.

We have to maneuver through these elements and get them to work for us as best we can. During COVID, our team applied for every type of grant and funding available, clawing to pull our business and teammates safely to the other side. We remained steadfast in the long Supperland buildout, optimistic that the challenges would pass. Social media could have been our undoing, as larger chain restaurants had money to boost posts; we didn't, but we managed to build it into a revenue driver with authenticity. Increased competition in our growing city could have run us out of business, but we elevated our concepts to entice the influx of foodies. The general trend of high staff turnover in our industry could have been our reason for failure, but we found a way to build trust and keep more staff. We opened Crêpe Cellar before the neighborhood was a safe bet, doing the best we could in a recession in an area with lower disposable income. In our favor, rent rates were less and there was a lot of used equipment available. Plus, we were downright scrappy with outreach efforts (remember those hours of sitting at that wooden barrel on gallery crawl nights?).

In any challenging situation, there's a choice to judge what comes as good or bad, or just allow it to be, and create something positive in its wake. Opportunities to flip situations are ever present, even if they're hiding behind a veil—preconceived notions, other people's opinions, traditional ways of doing things—at first. There is always an optimistic way of look-ing at a situation. If life gives you sour lemons—and it will—use the juice to make homemade limoncello, the zest to brighten up homemade ricotta, and the rinds to make a cocktail syrup. Positive energy bends circumstances toward prosperity.

In our very first group meeting for Leluia Hall, the upstairs mezzanine was of primary concern. It is a quirky spot to work with. Every time I walk in the building, I'm again surprised by how large the jutting mezzanine is. Poking out halfway up the enormous vertical height of the space, the mezzanine sits atop columns and doesn't extend all the way to the side walls. It wasn't the original prayer loft; it is what I'd call a "scar" to the original structure, put in place in the 1980s for the owner to have more retail space for his plant nursery and Christmas shop.

As much as it is a little jarring to look at, that extra square footage on the mezzanine is invaluable for a retail space or for increasing restaurant capacity. It seats about forty people, and it opens the door for us to have a private party area too. The former restaurant in the building did a simple wine setup on the mezzanine, but our restaurant group relies a lot on cocktail sales—and cocktails require wells and ice and refrigeration and, well, plumbing. We weren't set up for that.

During this first group meeting at Leluia Hall, we came up with a wild idea to make a "bridge bar" to span across the entryway, connecting the two sides of the mezzanine and giving us the chance to put in a fully operating, plumbed bar. The bartender would look out over the stairwell and across the mezzanine platform and be able to sling cocktails, wine, sodas, water, or whatever guests needed with ease. With that unusual bridge bar addition, our team would be able to serve a group of forty as a private party with all drinks being made upstairs instead of having to run them from the far back bar all the way through the dining room and up the steps, taking more time and decreasing the quality of the drinks.

Instead of fretting and getting stuck with constraints, we shifted into problem-solving mode to allow the absence of something (a fully functioning bar) to be created into exactly what we needed to provide the services we wanted.

Similarly, upon first opening Supperland, our trash buildup was higher than expected. We requested more trash pickups, but the service was unreliable, and no other waste management companies could assist. Jeff researched trash options and found unusual insights from the operations at Chick-fil-A. Many Chick-fil-A locations use a trash compacting system. After witnessing it firsthand, we invested in the same garbage compactor and a cardboard bailer for the Supperland trash area. The machines minimized the amount of space occupied by trash, so we weren't as desperate for the waste management company to pick up. With incredible integration into our business operations, we now use these bailer systems at several of our spots. Solving the one restaurant's trash problem helped our other businesses operate better too.

One of the most notable ways we've flipped a situation to our advantage is regarding my rigid diet for dealing with autoimmune issues. Even in what seems like an entirely detrimental situation (not being able to eat most of the food in our restaurants), I received abundant gifts. For example, cooking in a different way opened my eyes to a world of ingredients I had never used.

I add sweetness to a salad with dates or figs. I bake with a grain-free mixture of coconut flour, cassava flour, and tiger nut (a tuber, not a nut!) flour. Bone broth is a mainstay in my diet. I make crispy chicken skins in a pan as a snack. I've learned to make my own "cheese" from tapioca flour and nutritional yeast. I wring out steamed cauliflower in cheesecloth and mix it with cassava flour to make gnocchi, which I top with nightshade-free Bolognese. Baked coconut drizzled with maple syrup is a crunchy, sweet snack, and I make "white chocolate" from jarred coconut pulp, coconut oil, and honey powder. Plantain chips are a great grain-free alternative for nightshade-free guacamole with mango, onion, cilantro, and lime. Creamed avocado with maple syrup and lime is an outstanding replacement for key lime pie, and coconut aminos work perfectly in the place of soy sauce in a stir fry.

Experimenting with foods has encouraged both Jeff and me to pioneer greater mindfulness around food sensitivities that we're only too glad to extend to our guests. Many of our restaurant dishes are easily adaptable to a range of dietary restrictions, but our personal experience changed menus across all our restaurants in several ways.

We note gluten-free options on our menus, and if a certain category on a menu is inherently gluten-based, like pasta or bread, we bring in gluten-free substitutes. Our pasta at Ever Andalo is all homemade with white flour or semolina, but we have gluten-free pasta cooked in a separate pot available for guests. At Growlers Pourhouse, any of our sandwiches can be made with gluten-free bread. At Supperland's buffet brunch, we serve a gluten-free banana muffin, along with some gluten-free desserts like seasonally flavored macarons or chocolate–peanut butter mousse cups. Though Haberdish is known for its fried chicken, our team now grills chicken tenders for our gluten-sensitive guests.

The process by which we put menu items together has also become more thoughtful. Many higher-allergen ingredients are added at the end of the cooking process so they can be easily left off. For example, at

Supperland, the brussels sprouts are finished with toasted nuts—unless the diner requests no nuts. Leaving an allergen ingredient out is a nonissue for our kitchen; they are accustomed to it, and we make sure recipes and processes make it easy to execute.

We've also added a specific dish to Supperland's menu that was something I cooked every week for about two years during my elimination diet: blackened onions. The dish has just onions, olive oil, and salt—and it comes out bubbling to the table. Cooked in a cazuela, the onions sit in layered curves, so the tops of them blacken in the broiler in thin C shapes. Underneath the char, soft onions nearly melt into the oil; they're so velvety smooth. Maldon salt mixes with the sweet onion notes.

My food journey has brought about an incredibly unusual dessert item at Leluia Hall, too, an avocado lime pie. The genesis was my home recipe for avocado key lime pie, but it has been elevated to an entirely different level with the efforts of our pastry chef, Savannah Foltz. The outcome is tremendous and unlike any dessert I've seen on a steakhouse-like menu. It is free of the top allergens (except coconut) and sweetened only with honey, maple syrup, and dates. The tiger nut–date crust has a crumbly graham-cracker-like texture, and it's served with whipped coconut cream and mini kiwi gelée flowers.

All our restaurants have a "special diets" menu available upon request. Guests get an itemized list of which menu items fit in categories like gluten-free, dairy-free, nut-free, soy-free, and so on. Guests with these food sensitivities feel more comfortable—and, just as important to us, more welcome—to dine with us. They can eat in our restaurants without feeling burdensome. We're diligent to note that all our kitchens (to this point) have gluten in the kitchen, so we warn about cross-contamination, but our team is conscientious to ask about and work around serious sensitivities with great caution.

Besides my personal health journey impacting our menus, more than anything, by freeing my mind, I gained broader perspective as a restaurateur. I appreciate the layered elements of a dining experience beyond the food. I lead boldly on new projects and am unafraid of ambitious endeavors. I see unique potential in ingredients that chefs might not be accustomed to working with. I am better at my job because of what I went through and how I dug myself out.

Our ability to navigate these more challenging situations is about being action-oriented, goal-driven leaders who are unafraid of change—even having a willingness to create change and overcome problems by seeing the positives and using those challenges to position us in a better spot.

TEND TO FINANCES LIKE FIRE

Fire cooking at Supperland is an art. We have a fourteen-foot wood-fired grill—the showpiece of the dining room—also known as "Jeff's midlife crisis." Every day at two o'clock, one of our team members goes out to heave stacks of splintery wood onto a metal cart and push it up the zigzagging ramp to the side door of the dining room. The cart stops short of the door, as the heavy load has cracked our tile floors multiple times, so it is now banned from the interior of the building. With sling-like contraptions, the team drops armfuls of wood in front of the grill to be stowed in the cavity underneath.

When 3 p.m. hits, the team places log after log into the fire grill, hovering by warm charcoals pulled from the adjacent fire oven still smoldering from the night before. The wood begins to heat, tiny embers catching the stringy pieces of fraying wood. A grillman/woman confidently pushes the embers around with a rake to surround the wood with more heat. The flames begin to rise, and soon the entire fourteen feet of grill space is enlivened with a raging-mad fire, four feet high.

The art of cooking over fire, though, is knowing when the flames are ready to cook over and where the hot spots are. It's a constant tending. That knowledge comes with time. Our team starts the fires at 3 p.m. for a 5 p.m. service because the flames need to die down and the embers need to heat up. When the first guests arrive, the grill has reached that point, and the first steaks can hit the grates. There's a constant watch over the fire as the dining room fills, peaks, and then begins to slow. During that time, eyes are on the embers, reloading wood toward the back and shuffling the falling bits toward the front.

The art of keeping a fire is not much different from the art of keeping a business growing. We know the general strategies that work, but we have to stay with it.

We're relentless about keeping our fires. We're also relentless about managing the costs in our business. That scrupulous eye toward the financials has been more than critical in creating a thriving enterprise in an industry where most new ventures wash out early. The main reason restaurants fail is that margins are so tight. That means while a guest may spend $60 for a dinner, we don't keep all that money. About $20 goes toward buying the ingredients for the food, another $25 goes toward the people who made the food in our kitchen, and then we have rent/mortgage, marketing dollars, and utilities to pay for. By then, we're left with a maximum of about $6 in profit. As I said, the margins are tight. That means one bad week can start the burial process. Several bad weeks in a row, and you're losing savings. Within a month, the business is unprofitable and possibly unsalvageable. The tight margins in this industry don't leave much room for error or uncontrollable circumstances.

Jeff and I laugh about how good our restaurants are at creating sales revenue—some of our spots are powerhouses—but that doesn't mean profit. In a tight-margin business, your job is greatly about carving profits off those revenue streams. If you have a sandwich shop that sells $10 sandwiches and you sell 100,000 of them over a year, or about 275 a day, the business will bring in $1 million in revenue. If yours is a typical restaurant making 3–5 percent margins, then you're spending between $950,000 and $970,000 of that $1 million—on lease payments, food and supplies, staffing, insurance, permits, utilities, and so on—to keep your business running. That means you're making just $30,000–$50,000 in profit for the year. It's a lot of work for not much reward. Plus, if you make a $40,000 mistake or mishaps add up (equipment failure, leaks, natural disasters, HVAC issues, employee legal issues, whatever), your entire next year will be spent digging out of that hole.

As part of the tending process, we know the ebbs and flows of our seasons. Summers tend to be slower, while February, March, and October through December have super high sales. January and September are our slowest months. It's been like this every year for us. But unfavorable numbers not related to seasons don't stay that way long. We immediately seek to remedy food costs, sourcing difficulties, overtime pay, and anything else that adversely impacts the health of our business. That's the importance of that sway and adroitness we've discussed. We move quickly because we have to—tending keenly to tiny details that have wide impact.

When we launched Ever Andalo in March of 2022, we had a mushroom tortellini dish with mixed mushrooms, truffle oil, shaved Parmigiano Reggiano, porcini cream, and greens. The flavors melded with creaminess and subtle umami notes. Each tortellini was only about an inch in diameter, and we had precisely twelve to a plate. From the very beginning, the dish was challenging. One, the tortellini was handmade, so the item had high labor costs. Two, it didn't hold heat well because the filled pasta was so small and the pasta was separated on the plate with little saucing. That brought guest complaints. Three, the tortellini wasn't difficult to make, but the job required training. We had a very particular fold that twisted where the pasta was connected. Only a tiny amount of filling could fit in each one. Too much filling and the tortellini would burst in the boiling water, too little and we'd lose the mushroom flavor. The pasta had to be just the right moisture level to be pressed together at the seams—something we achieved with spritzer water bottles.

As we were running up to the opening, I spent several days in the kitchen with my twelve-year-old daughter—partly to train teammates on the pasta fold but also because we needed tortellini for service, and the two of us knew how to make it. We didn't have enough other teammates trained yet.

As our opening months went by, the challenges with our tortellini continued to surface. We weren't making labor costs. Guests complained about the dish being cold. We lost a significant number of labor-intensive tortellini that burst in the boiling water. The challenges prompted us to consider removing the item from the menu, but it was an excellent dish. We wanted to find a way to get it right.

The solution came in a single letter. We changed from tortellini to tortelloni, the latter being about double the size of the former. With a filled pasta about two inches wide, we moved from twelve to a plate to nine. The tortelloni was slightly easier for staff to make because the larger size made them easier to handle, and they rarely burst in the boiling water. Plus, putting three fewer on each plate dropped the necessary yield by a quarter. With a larger bite, the heat held longer, and the mushroom flavor came through better by having more filling.

Mindful tending to tiny factors as we conceptualize menu items and openness to making changes to dishes or processes that aren't working perfectly, both forms of careful tending, make a big difference in the success of a restaurant. This heightened strategic thinking across a whole menu and a whole business, from food to labor costs, shifts a high-risk business to a more manageable spot.

The food industry has morphed since we started in 2009, impacting how we manage food costs. Guests have much higher expectations for everything. Guests want local. They want farm fresh. And they want it every day of the year. They also want consistency, and they want to have their favorite items always available. Charlotte's tremendous growth has brought in a new population from larger cities like New York and Chicago. Some of the newbies to Charlotte are affluent, and they may not be as price conscious when it comes to dining out. They're also looking for local spots—not chains—to spend their money. For the most part, so long as we continue to meet the rising expectations, guests have been willing to pay to dine with us. That's been helpful because, to keep up with supply chain issues and price increases on some primary ingredients, we've had no choice but to raise menu prices.

Food costs in a restaurant typically run between 30 and 35 percent. That means that of all of our operating expenses, 30–35 percent is used to buy the ingredients that go into our final dishes. And there's a big difference between having food costs at 30 percent versus 35 percent. If a restaurant is 5 percent profitable overall with food costs at 35 percent, bringing their food costs down to 30 percent will double their profits.

Our team monitors our food costs on a weekly basis through manager reports. If food costs are higher than normal, our managers figure out why so we can fix the imbalance quickly. If we serve 2 ounces of a creamy triple cream cheese on a charcuterie board and the cost rises tremendously because the cheesemaker's supply dropped, we might adjust to put 1.8 ounces on the plate. It seems small, but where margins are tight and dozens of charcuterie boards go out to tables each night, that small adjustment can make an unprofitable item profitable again. Our chefs sometimes hear in advance about rising prices, and we're proactive to preempt the impact. If chefs hear that beef prices are going up, we're ready to adjust the menu— whether with a price change or a serving size change—to maintain our average 30 to 35 percent food costs.

Our strict "shelf-to-sheet" inventory methods help maintain our food costs too. When our team is counting the inventory in the walk-in fridge, for example, they look at what's on the shelf and write the count down on a sheet. The *shelf* always tells us what we have—you can see it physically in front of you. So we go down the shelf and count eggs, cream, half and half, and lemon juice, and we mark it on the sheet. If you instead go from the sheet to the shelf, you might gloss over something that's actually sitting in inventory on the shelf—and it might be sitting there ready to spoil or go stale. Good inventory numbers help our kitchen know what we need to order and what we need to use up. If we have an excess of something, we work that ingredient into a special to keep waste down.

Taking this tending game to another level, we get together with a small group for quarterly strategic meetings to step back and look broadly at each restaurant and the business as a whole. There are lessons from one concept we can pull over to another. There are negotiating tactics we can use to improve all our cost savings. There are small changes that, when implemented across multiple restaurants, have great impact. Tending to the business from a different vantage point, a wider vantage point, has saved us tens of thousands of dollars over the course of a year.

We watch over our costs and our profits every day—tending to our finances like fire. It's the difference in reaping versus draining in a low-margin business.

CRAFT CONSISTENCY

Each of our restaurants is open anywhere from thirty to over forty hours a week. Putting out thousands of dishes each day and being consistent with all these items throughout the day, with different menus and different team-mates, is an incredible act, and an act that when done mindfully, helps us mitigate risk. The task of food quality falls on our chefs, and while we always have things to work on and improve upon, they've done an incredible job.

When a dish like our Ever Andalo gnocchi goes out to a table, the weighted amount of gnocchi is 4.5 ounces. A smooth, ovular ricotta quenelle gets placed just askew with a scattering of herbs over the food. The sauce is scarlet red, the result of those canned San Marzano tomatoes we import from Italy. It's the same every time. Guests return for the consistent flavors, and our business needs that consistency to temper risk.

We take a few steps to maintain food consistency, and some of these seem like obvious guide rails, but they aren't always easy to enact.

First, we use accurate written recipes that can be prepared by multiple people. It seems standard, but you'd be surprised by how many dishes in restaurant kitchens don't follow recipes to a T. A "winging-it" style of cooking creates not only inconsistencies in the flavor of the dish but also in food costs. We allowed some of this rogue style for years, but the inconsistencies added up. Now that the business is even more challenging with rising food and labor costs, there's no room for regular inaccuracies.

Second, we get everyone on the same page from the moment we begin training for the opening of a restaurant. Everyone on the team knows what dishes are supposed to taste like and look like. Photos of plated and garnished dishes guide the kitchen team—from the sear of a protein to the height of the dish to garnish placement. This is not something we've perfected, but it's where we aim.

Next, in some cases, we use pH meters for cocktails to ensure sugar and acidity levels are balanced and consistent. Our team has standard recipes for everything from homemade tonic water to syrups, garnishes, and final cocktails. We don't want bartenders making an old-fashioned the way they make one at home. We want our old-fashioned to be the same every time a customer orders it at our restaurant, regardless of who's behind the bar. When guests know they're going to get a great drink every time, they return for it repeatedly.

Our team has weekly scheduled tastings that rotate from one kitchen to the next. In these tastings, we're able to dial in on items that aren't being executed properly. One of the most difficult parts of managing consistency is that Jeff and I aren't able to be at every one of our restaurants, tasting every item every week. It's physically not possible. So we've enrolled managers to report back on their meals out at our places, and this gives us more eyeballs and more taste buds out there keeping our flavors, plating, and service in line.

Structured menus have assisted with consistency too. We understand the allure of creatively changing the daily menu at a restaurant. There's so much creative potential for chefs. It can be fun for regulars too. A seasonal plump squash with a curvy neck can be roasted and puréed and stirred with cream into a soup topped with fresh local herbs. The carrots poking from the farmer's basket can be simply grilled and maybe topped with a carrot top pesto for a perfect root-to-stem dish. Seasonal sunchokes are excellent fried; they get all crispy, and with those lovely nutty flavors, they make a great appetizer or a garnish on top of a protein. The options are endless with a farmer's basket of goods; creativity can run wild. But our approach is different. Seasonal ingredients hit our "specials" menu. But we do a *lot* of research and menu development prior to the restaurant's opening to ensure that the menu is balanced, stays consistent, the dishes fit the brand, ingredients can be cross-utilized, and that every item plays a part in the restaurant's storytelling.

We'll modify a menu item if the feedback isn't positive on it. Sometimes dishes do really well in our taste-testing process, but then, for various reasons, they don't fly with the guests. If our team has a hard time with consistency in preparing the dish or in sourcing the ingredients, we'll consider making changes. Otherwise, because of the multidirectional thought that goes into the menu planning, we keep the framework of the offering at each spot pretty much the same. We get better at making the same things. And favorite mainstay items drive guests back in the door, increasing repeat visits.

There are challenges to this approach. Keeping a consistent menu can feel stifling for chefs or regular customers. Chefs like to be creative. Regulars like to have some variety to choose from. So we have areas on the menus where chefs can create specials. These spots are often structured so that the menu retains balance and stays on brand. At Haberdish, we regularly have one special in each category: hot side, cold side, entrée, daily pickle, and sometimes a sundae. At Growlers Pourhouse, we switch out ice cream flavors, a soup of the day, and oyster varietals. At Ever Andalo, we have a daily crudo, daily pasta, cannoli, and often an ice cream or sorbet. It's not that the chefs can't do other types of specials, but these frameworks keep their processes consistent, and they have clear buckets to fill for each service.

Just like we do for food, we prepare our team properly for service so our level of hospitality is consistent. If expectations are set high, even if our team falls a little short, we're still operating above the level guests might expect. Each restaurant has a manual—a step-by-step look at service points to communicate that every detail matters. Service points direct servers on how quickly to visit a table and what to attend to, including silverware switch-outs or what serving utensils to bring to the table for certain menu items. At Supperland's brunch buffet, servers are to note when guests rise from the table to visit the buffet so they can switch out plates and silverware, along with a quick refold of napkins. Trainees learn the menu, how to speak about the menu, how to replace silverware, and how to properly set plates down. At Supperland, plates are turned toward the guest so the artwork on the plate is upright. And servers are trained to avoid "backhand service," so they deliver items to the table with their palm facing the guest rather than the back of their hand facing the guest.

Service consistencies can be as simple as having a standard way that a table is set. When we were opening Ever Andalo, we must have gone back and forth fifteen times trying to decide if we should set the table with a butter knife. The thing is, as small as that seems, it's critical to set both the guest and the server up for great service. To watch the unfolding of our quick restaurant turnover from Crêpe Cellar to Ever Andalo, I had invited a local writer to follow along with us. When the story was published, the second leading line read: "The butter knife rests diagonally across the bread plate. This may not matter to you, but it does to Jamie Brown." We practiced and discussed alternatives and hemmed and hawed, but in the end, at opening, the butter knife was indeed placed across the plate. At Supperland, when the team is opening for service, someone goes around the room with a measuring tape to check that our tables are 18.5 inches away from the back of the pew. We've found that to be the perfect distance for an average person to feel comfortable in their seat with the table at the proper place in front of them. It's about having standards to guide the team and setting expectations that create a repeatable experience.

Because Jeff and I have so far created only single-location restaurant concepts, it's a little easier to maintain consistency. Our challenges come in making sure that the food, drinks, service, and experience feel consistent from one guest visit to the next. We want people to know what to expect and for our team to deliver that. We aim for repeatability in our dining room. But that doesn't mean we aren't up for the spontaneous.

Elements of surprise in new cocktails, pie flavors, a new bottle of wine, or seasonal specials help. Even more important for service, though, is the balance between servers knowing their stuff and bringing the fluidity of personality to the service. We train our team to be educated and well-versed on the menu and specific steps of service: when silverware switch-outs happen, when to offer a second round of drinks, when to clear plates, how long to wait to check on a table, and knowledge about ingredient sourcing and cooking processes—all these are meant to be consistent from one server to the next. With that foundation, we then count on the server's personality and rapport with the guest to mold an entirely different experience every time. This unique relationship between a server and a table is hard to quantify, but it always makes dining out a little more fun, a little more colorful, a little more *delicious*.

SET UP SYSTEMS TO WIN

At the beginning, when we set any of our restaurants up, in our business plan, we run our initial planning numbers and forecasting to aim for a 12–15 percent profit. It's ambitious, but it helps us manage risk.

Every percent matters in this business. With a 10 percent margin, if food costs unexpectedly rise that year, we might lose 1 percent of our margins. If labor costs increase (as they have over the past five years), or if our team relies too much on overtime labor (which is more expensive), that might take away another 1 percent. Suddenly, our planned 10 percent margin becomes 8 percent (we've lost 2 percent of our margins, which is 20 percent less profit for the overall business). That's a big swing. For us, it's a constant tending process to carve out profits and hold on to every percent we can of our incoming revenue. Luckily, there are tangible actions that have made a difference.

Let's look closer at how we create a conservative revenue forecast in our business plan. We crunch numbers that anticipate lower revenue than what we actually think we can achieve, which requires playing with the numbers in our spreadsheet. We might really believe we can make a $4 million business, but our financial plan will be pieced together for a mere $3 million business. We won't sign a lease unless we can make the business work with that lower $3 million number.

Here's how we do that: While we might someday imagine having a busy lunch crowd where we serve up five-inch-high burgers with melty, gooey cheese, pops of purple pickled onions, and a bright, zesty sauce, the envisioning must wait. We remove any expected lunch revenue. Same goes for the three-person-deep bar where bartenders are passing around fizzy cocktails dressed with citrus and leafy garnishes. We'll even drop the number of tables or seats we plan to have, creating a floor plan that is spacious, not tightly packed. While we dream that guests will spend $100 on average per person to get their pink lobster with bubbling butter pour-overs and caviar setups with fresh-made blinis and crème fraîche, the projection gets tempered to a lower price point per guest, say, $85 a person. We temper our forecast so we can plan ahead for lean years, pandemics, recessions, or any other slow season. Now we're set up to buck the 3–5 percent profit trend in our industry.

Those conservative binds we place ourselves in during the planning process set us up for a more profitable business for the years that follow.

Another way we tee the business up to win is that from the first stage of our buildouts, our restaurant group holds a "Not Closing" principle to guide our setup. We focus on quality by installing sturdy and well-sealed flooring, strong HVAC systems, and top-notch equipment in the kitchen. Investing in high-quality infrastructure allows our ongoing operations to be less consumed with fixing problems. We set the restaurant up to hopefully never have to close for repairs.

We choose tile over hardwood floors, if possible, because if wood floors need refinishing, the restaurant has to close for multiple shifts. We keep extra parts for essential items like our doughnut machine—when it breaks, the shop could be closed for days if we have to await parts. We have an extra water heater we can pull parts from for any of the places. The walk-in fridge at Supperland has a generator to avoid food waste in case of a power outage. These are all things that can shut down operations. That "Not Closing" precautionary mentality safeguards against nights with zero revenue.

A big part of winning—beyond setting systems up favorably for the ongoing profit game—is setting the business up to thrive in the space itself with a mortgage or lease that makes financial sense and positions the business for long-term survival.

At Supperland, we have a twenty-year lease, with the rent bumping up 2.5 percent every year. Plus, we have three different options to exit through those two decades. We will build up our Supperland business on our corner lot, serving plate after plate of fire-cooked steaks topped with lump crab and loaf after loaf of homemade porridge bread with our hot pink beet butter. People will edge in and out of our weekend brunch buffet, filling up with homemade eggs Benedict, tea sandwiches, and our seasonal jello. All along that daily dance of hospitality, we'll understand that rent is rising consistently each year to cover inflation and growth in the neighborhood. But we expect this rise. We know what's coming, and that knowledge decreases our risk.

At Haberdish, we went about the lease a little differently. We pay rent on a percentage of sales. As our CEO/CFO, Jeff is very clear that, in general, he does not like this sort of arrangement or other stipulations where we share our revenue numbers with a landlord. It makes later negotiations with the landlord difficult and lopsided, since they have your numbers, but you don't have theirs. Then potentially negotiating to buy the building becomes dependent on the cash flow of the restaurant rather than on the real estate market itself. Real estate cash flows are simple, cut and dry, and emotionless.

Despite Jeff's disdain for percent rent, our Haberdish lease made a lot of sense at the time. It was a trade-off, because none of us knew the coming impact of the Charlotte light-rail system that was soon to run through the NoDa neighborhood. Our landlord needed a way for the market price to adjust, and we needed it to adjust without a gigantic jump in our lease. We were given a very low price to start, but our landlord has profited greatly from these terms because our restaurant continues to thrive. The most beneficial part for us is that the landlord was willing to do a long-term lease because we conceded to do a percent-rent format—and the longevity of the lease is always of utmost importance to us.

Some people think seven years is a long lease for a restaurant. It is not. Let's say a restaurant has a six-year lease with no option to renew and no agreed-upon rise in rent at that time. Just as the business has grown enough to become profitable, the tenant is backed into a corner and at the mercy of the landlord's changes in terms. The common practice for landlords is to raise the rent to "market rate" for a space, typically much higher than the tenant is accustomed to paying. The restaurant operators can look for another space, but so much of what makes a restaurant is tied up in its location, its feel, its local guests, and its staff. All of that is at risk the moment the business is required to move to another spot. Facing the inevitable rise in lease rates, many restaurants just close.

A landlord, of course, prefers a shorter-term lease; in just a handful of years, they can increase their income without changing a thing. But Jeff and I won't sign a lease unless we have options to re-sign at specific, predetermined increases. This mitigates our risk.

Our leases are a little different from one place to the next, but here are some key components that we want in a lease:

- We look for a twenty-year term. Twenty years is long enough for us to build the business with regulars, become profitable, and even generate enough profits to invest in the people, the design/decor, or the real estate itself.

- We predetermine all rent increases over the course of the long-term lease; that way, we know when rents will rise.

- We make certain we have the first right of refusal to purchase the property. In this case, if the owner decides to sell the real estate, they are obligated to give us (as the tenant) the chance to buy the property before it goes on the market. Restaurateurs don't make nest eggs by selling food. They make nest eggs by owning property. If our restaurant business is a success, we want to be in a position to reinvest our money into the real estate itself.

- We ensure a way out. An exit strategy from any lease is critical in an unpredictable industry. Even if breaking the lease requires a certain fee or a three-month notice, we have it in writing. While we haven't needed to rely on this clause to date, it gives us a little more control should a business not become profitable quickly enough.

Generally, the industry average for renting a restaurant space falls around 6–9 percent of the business's targeted revenue number. We negotiate with landlords to get to a lower number: around 5 percent (including any taxes, homeowners association fees, or condo fees, depending on the space's requirements). If we have a very busy, high-revenue restaurant, that 5 percent lease rate is easier to hit.

Also keep in mind that besides the actual rent payment to the landlord, other items can be negotiated. There's room to negotiate the lease term length, HVAC needs (sometimes a landlord will help install new units), water bills, and a new roof (landlords often will pitch in to make their building sounder). You could also ask for more TI (tenant improvement money). If the landlord offers $15K of TI versus $50K, that can make a big difference for a start-up restaurant. We ask for everything up front to give ourselves a better chance of getting it. This has become easier for us as we've had more success (because landlords want a consistently paying tenant), but any business owner should speak up from the get-go to get more from the landlord.

This is a risky business, and in any risky business, diversification will mitigate your risk. By positioning the business to purchase the real estate, the concept's longevity is more assured. That's an investment to help ensure personal financial security in the future as well.

In 2015, when we were leasing the Crêpe Cellar and Growlers Pourhouse units, Jeff approached our landlord to see if their group would be interested in selling the two side-by-side spaces to us. Jeff was look-ing down the road and knew that for restaurants to ensure money in the long haul, we'd have to make a real estate play. Restaurants come and go. Sometimes you can sell a restaurant concept, but you're much more certain to sell a building—especially in an up-and-coming or established neigh-borhood. If we could use the cash flow from our restaurants to purchase the property, we could secure a physical asset for our company. The build-ing would come with a tenant (us) already in place to pay the mortgage, and we'd own real estate, which generally increases in value over time.

It was absolute fortuitous timing. Our landlord, Red Partners, happened to be looking to free up cash, so they were open to the sale. Their asking price was fair, no gouging or haggling. They sold us the Crêpe Cellar/

Growlers Pourhouse spaces, and there we were, just a few years into our business, with the comfort of a piece of real estate—not only to protect our restaurants' locations but also to give our family greater security. We had solid ground on which to build.

A business of any kind requires managing risk. The secrets to success vary from one industry to the next, but what's clear is that you can't do all the exciting, fun stuff if you don't have a strong foundation set underneath.

SERVING SPOON: How well do you know your numbers? Can you set yourself up early with strategic plans that give you room for shortcomings along the way?

BUILD ON BELIEF

Keep cooking.

Jeff and I have been in this business now for over fifteen years. It's different from what I thought it would be. I imagined long, difficult hours, being always on your feet, people yelling at each other, and no one able to calmly or lovingly succeed. The tension, I thought, was necessary for success, and the long hours too—especially if we owned multiple places. I did not foresee calm. I did not foresee creativity or peace or beauty. I did not foresee camaraderie or balance, teamwork or incredible friendships. I did not see the possibility of working in tandem with other restaurant groups to build our city's dining scene. But now that we are in it, these are the things that fill our lives.

It has taken us time to get here, but with a team of people who care, who work in balance, and who communicate with authenticity and patience, we have a great work-life balance. We do work a lot, but because we love what we do and we love our team, we are at ease.

Our restaurants are unique. We develop our concepts in a really different way. A lot of people who open an independent restaurant want to honor a type of cuisine they grew up with, or recipes from their family, or maybe there's a food trend that they want to bring forth in a restaurant. Our restaurants have very much followed our journey as a couple—as we grow and change and raise a family, call the South our home, and experience life. Each one is different, and they're special and personal to us in part because they tell our story.

Each of our restaurant concepts is a dot on our timeline together. Each spot marks significant happenings in our personal world. We experience food and drink ourselves and then curate particular elements to offer that enjoyment to our guests.

Why would anyone want to open a restaurant? The stakes are incredibly high. By some accounts, 60 percent of restaurants will not survive their first year, and 80 percent won't make it past year four. Operators hope for slim profits—with long working hours. Managers must trust new hires to handle guest experiences and interactions. The business is subject to rising food costs, high labor costs, changing economic climates, and sourcing issues. Criticism is high in this industry—a new concept can get slashed down before it's given a shot to thrive. Stereotypes of angry chefs and unkind kitchen environments abound.

But we understand the allure. We love this business.

We see another side of it, one that promises growth and education for the three hundred–some people on our team, one that allows us to create unique destinations within our city, a newer city that relies greatly on its dining scene to build the local economy, create jobs, spur tourism, and inspire local culture. It's a business that's thoughtful and mindful of waste and that develops a culture of love and support for many who need it. We see an industry that makes guests happy with creative, delicious food and drink, providing settings for celebrations, memories, and joyous occasions.

Where else can a person walk into a building and taste, touch, smell, hear, and see—and then witness the show-like course of service as servers dance from table to table, chefs sprinkle and dash, and hosts warmly welcome? The guest, too, becomes a part of the theatrics when they savor the food and settle into the satisfaction of being well-fed and cared for. There's nothing like the artistry of the restaurant business, catering to every sense through the dining experience.

Jeff and I went on that trip all those years ago, hoping to find ourselves. It took us (okay, *me*) a minute to figure it out, but we did find what we were looking for, and that trip spawned the dream we still chase today. We just had to green-light the idea and then build that dream into something tangible and resilient.

The process starts with being willing to risk where you are because you see something more or something better. You step forward. And from there, you don't stop until you get where you envision going. Every obstacle that pops up, you find your way through, over, or around. When something doesn't work, you try a different way. When you fall, you rise. When you need to evolve, you stay open to it. When the load is too heavy, you lean on those around you.

Jeff and I have taken many risks, and taking risks can be scary. But humans are at their best when we're unafraid, so I like to tackle fears head-on, whispering things like: "I see you, *fear of failure*. I see you, *fear of what people will think*. I see you, *worry about the future*." I recognize these feelings and acknowledge them—sometimes even out loud. I sit with these fears and just look at them without letting them overwhelm me. When the time is right, I lift my hands in front of me and lightly press that whole batch of worry aside. It scoots off to the right. The worries are still there, but now I look at something else: the most positive image of my vision.

I see what I want to see. With clarity and in full color, I imagine who is there, what is happening, what we've achieved, and how it feels to be in the moment of success. I sense the tastes, smells, and feelings. I envision the situation going well and that I'm happy, overjoyed, and full of gratitude in the moment. I stay with these imaginings as long as it feels real and authentic and brings me happiness to think about them.

Then I ask for my vision. I ask for it from myself, and from the Universe, God, Source of all that is. I believe that it is real, that it is my life, that it is coming my way.

When I'm done thinking about it and asking for my dream, I return to reality.

Of course, reality often looks very different from what I just saw behind my eyes. I've been there many times, and it's okay. It means I've got an adventurous journey ahead, and that I'll become what I need to become in just the right time.

Taking risks is what moves us forward, both as individuals and as humanity more broadly. In our world, restaurants cannot become better entities unless we take risks and do things in a unique way. Restaurants cannot be great places to have careers unless we think differently. Food sourcing cannot improve unless we take new paths. Experiences cannot become richer unless we risk trying novel things.

Risks don't always pan out, of course. Sometimes Jeff and I have fallen flat on our faces. Aside from the restaurants and concepts that never were, different television production companies pitched us out four times to do a TV show, and none of the concepts got picked up by networks. In each TV pitch, the timing wasn't right, we weren't what the networks were looking for, or budgets wouldn't allow for the filming costs. It was a hopeful dream, and one we'd have to await fruition of for more than six years. Aside from those failed pitches, we lost dozens of employees and some long-time customers when we transitioned Crêpe Cellar to Ever Andalo. We've launched menu items, like our bologna sandwich at Growlers Pourhouse, that we thought would be super interesting to guests, but they didn't get received past a tight cultish following.

As much as we've succeeded, we've failed. But through it all, we hold a vision toward a positive future and maintain a belief that life happens for us, not to us. This positive mindset has encouraged us to continue to risk, to continue to try new things, to get back up when we fall, to learn to change, and to try again and again to chase the results we want. We keep building on our belief.

BUILDING LEGO CASTLES IN THE SKY

Someone once said to me, "Wow, everything you all touch turns to gold."

That might have been how it seemed, but that was because people only heard about our successes. Our "failures" and missteps were never very public, but they were very much present and impactful in our lives. Haberdash House was one failed attempt, but we had another hit even harder.

After we opened Reigning Doughnuts in 2017, we were still looking to grow. Near our house and adjacent to the north-south light-rail line in South End was an old trolley barn. When our kids were babies, we'd push them over in strollers to the Saturday morning farmer's market held inside the gigantic space. Rail tracks poked up through the concrete, and large crane-like yellow arms—that once hoisted trolleys up for fixing—hung above.

The farmer's market brought mom-and-pop vendors selling handmade soaps embedded with dried flowers, flaky pastries with local grains and fruits and nuts, jewelry with colorful beads hung from miniature trees, and fresh cheese wheels cut into triangles with jagged crumbles splayed on trays. A local coffee shop showed off brews with latte art, boasting pris-tinely designed leaflets.

The developer hoped to reinvigorate the trolley barn as part of the Atherton Mills project, where hundreds of apartments were being built around the restored former textile mills. They hoped to find a single tenant able to pay higher rent—rates that weren't feasible for the pop-up artisan market tenants, even with combined efforts. Conversations started quickly with the developer. A grand vision was formulating in our minds, and the developer was interested in our unique proposition, which created a second-floor mezzanine with a deck extending out toward the city, with views that could remain intact with the fortuitous light-rail track shooting toward the Charlotte skyline. The hybrid concept we proposed included a full-scale restaurant with a market threaded throughout the space in kitchen prep stations—like the well-known Italian market Eataly, but on a smaller scale and not focused exclusively on Italian food. The kitchen prep areas would support our restaurant in the trolley barn, but they would also support our other concepts by providing homemade prepped ingredients like pastas, sauces, syrups, and baked goods. Our restaurants could expand menu offerings and make more homemade items—the way we liked to do it. Then, guests could shop in our market-like space and buy prepared foods for at-home use.

Down one aisle, we would sell kitchen gear: aprons, high-end cookware, and beautiful dishes and cookbooks. On the back wall, refrigerators would store sheet-pan dinners that people could buy and pop in the oven at home. The kitchen prep stations would offer fresh grated cheeses like our family's favorite, Pecorino Romano, and fresh sliced meats like prosciutto, salami, or speck. A large U-shaped bar in the middle of the market would seat guests for lunch.

The plan was coming to life beautifully—so beautifully, in fact, that Jeff and I built a Lego scale model of it to help visualize the stations, the flow, the mezzanine, and the restaurant itself. The color-coded structures delineated spaces and created aisles, seating areas, line queuing, and even glassed-in areas where guests could see ingredients like fresh pasta being made. Our model was constructed within mere inches of the actual space.

For more than six months, we negotiated back and forth with the developers, arriving at a plan to pay $28/square foot—a higher price than they'd expected to get for the awkwardly large space. We were willing to pay it based on revenue forecasts and the creative concept that was blooming in our minds. We also knew that other spaces in the area were climbing up to $45–$50 per square foot at the time.

We sent a signed letter of intent for the trolley barn space, eager to move forward with the project and mindful of its likely long lead time. A month passed. Then another. Then the developer came back to us and turned us down. They'd found another tenant willing to pay nearly double what we'd offered.

After a year of pouring ourselves into this innovative project, the loss hurt. Every time I walk by that space, even still, I see our Lego model in my head and note the similarities to the layout that's there now. There's a mezzanine, a second-level deck, a restaurant, and even a large bar when you enter from the longer side of the building.

I don't blame any of them. As a landlord, they were right to seek other potential tenants. In the end, an awesome local brewery opened in the space, bringing hundreds of people together each night. Losses feel harsher when you're passionate about something, but the point of going after a dream is to go after it with everything you have. Projects don't always turn out, but that uncertainty doesn't mean we don't pour our whole hearts into them.

As the weeks of disappointment passed, Jeff and I began to let the idea float away. We stopped talking about our hundreds of ideas for hospitality and goods and experiences we would have had there. We no longer curved our neighborhood walk to pass in front of the trolley barn so we could sit on a nearby wall and dream. The children slowly disassembled our Lego model to build imaginary cities and treehouses and flying cars.

As that door closed, I flipped my work notebook to a clean page. It was time to get back up. Our attention shifted toward the unusual church space in Plaza Midwood—the one that sneakily sat a little outside possibility until all the zoning and parking and structural issues were tended to. It was time to turn our energy toward Supperland, at the time, our next new thing.

GROWING DREAMS

Every week, I run a four-mile route down a trail next to the Charlotte light-rail heading southbound. I'm one of those people who absorbs energy from liveliness around me, and the light-rail, with the thousands of apartments and dense, young population, well, it lifts me. I get to the light-rail pretty easily; just about five blocks from my house, I cross South Boulevard and ramp down a brick-lined cement path onto the rail trail. Businesses dot every street—quick-serve restaurants, nail salons, retail shops—and I marvel that they stay afloat through all the changes we've seen in the last fifteen years.

Two blocks up, on this day, I looked to my left, like I always did, and located the spot. Across a parking lot and buzzing South Boulevard, there had been a two-story brick building with a black awning. And it was no longer there—someone had physically moved the building.

It wasn't a special building to me. Just a red brick building with tall parapets sitting atop. The windows were cool, like all old windows are. Just different. The brickwork around them was noticeably more crafted, with broad wood beams spanning above them. Knowing more now, that building was the grocery store that served the Atherton Mill village and surrounding Dilworth and Wilmore neighborhoods. This was where the locals shopped for goods for their kitchens at the turn of the century.

So, back to the someone who physically moved that building.

It was us.

We got into the restaurant business to create fun, curated hospitality experiences for guests to enjoy. But somehow, in the midst of wanting to build these special, one-of-a-kind places, we got into the business of salvaging old spaces to bring forth hospitality concepts. I guess when you're on a journey and you're listening to the things that light you up, you end up on some pretty spectacular paths.

It's hard to say exactly when this project became "ours." A friend of Jeff's was interested in moving the historic building to a different lot. He had commissioned the engineering work to see if the building could actually be transported, and the good news was that it could. The bad news was that the lot where he wanted to move it had a very steep grade. It was too steep to accept the building. So he came to us in passing and said, "The only other nearby lot I could see this going is right there." He pointed to the parking lot next to our Leluia Hall church project. Our parking lot was just a couple blocks away from where the historic grocery store sat.

Those were the seeds that would require a very arduous process in getting the city and community to say yes to the project.

There were hoops to jump through to rezone our parking lot, lose the twelve parking spaces, and put a building in its place. While the majority of Charlotteans were in favor of the project, a handful of nearby neighbors were vehemently opposed. They didn't want us to lose our parking lot and inevitably push more patrons to street parking in the neighborhood. That opposition meant that when it was time for us to go in front of the city council, we had dissenters in the room speaking against the project.

Queue the flashback to when we first tried to open a restaurant in Dilworth—Haberdash House. The criticism. The anger. The personal attacks. Remember we vowed to ourselves to never open a restaurant in historic Dilworth? Now, here we were, headlining toward two projects on the same block in that community.

A few things worked in our favor, like the fact that we were located just a couple blocks from the light-rail and a massive public transportation network. We were also zoned in a pedestrian-friendly area where the city was trying to encourage walking, biking, and rideshare. The parking lot had once had a home on it, plus, the building was designated a historic landmark in the county. Those were the positives. But of course, with any large, impactful project, opinions were not unified. It took multiple city council meetings, fighting through the historic district commission, and getting through a very tight vote count to shake out the results we were after.

In the habit of looking at the positives, the rigorous process had its bright spots. We were able to connect with new friends and supporters, some of whom had much more powerful voices than ours. We were able to compromise on some issues that, in the end, would make our project better. Also, we stood up to save a historic landmark in our fast-moving city—in itself, that landmark was worth fighting for. Last, ironically, all the attention through the controversy brought a lot of eyeballs our way. People learned about what we were doing, what we stood for, and what we were trying to create. The public visibility was valuable.

Eventually the rezoning passed, and on September 12, 2024, the Leeper-Wyatt building was transported 750 feet out its back parking lot. It traveled up the hill on Cleveland Avenue, making a sharp right (slowly) into our parking lot, to its new home adjacent to the Leluia Hall site.

Moving day was sheer celebration. We got out to the grounds around 7:30 a.m.; the moving guys were ready to go. They had staged the building on the edge of the property to enter Cleveland Avenue that morning at 9 a.m. At that point, the street was shut down for the building to pass. The street's edges began filling up with people. Neighbors walked down the hill with folding chairs. A local news station came out to do their morning show from our site. We set up a tent with complimentary doughnuts from Reigning Doughnuts—one a champagne doughnut, the other chocolate with miniature construction cones as confetti. The street was lined with baby strollers and young people from South End who had been following the story and didn't want to miss "moving day." Adding to the celebration, the entire third-grade class from Dilworth Elementary—a school located just a few blocks away—walked to the site as an educational field trip to support their studies of historic landmarks.

There were pauses along the way as the building slowly progressed up the street. Power lines had to be lifted. Others had to be dropped. Some trees needed to be cut back. But the Leeper-Wyatt building found a new home that day. Someday we'll open a new concept in there too.

And how about those neighbors who hated the idea, who stood in strong opposition to the project to save the Leeper-Wyatt building? I hope nothing more than that they come enjoy the space. I hope they come see the beautiful place and team and menu that we put together. We built this for them too. I get it. Change is hard. Everyone likes to protect and hold on to what they have. It's hard to be open to different things sometimes. I know now that their refutes forced that project to be better. Whether they wanted to be a part of the initiative or not, that adversity was not wasted.

Now when people drive on Cleveland Avenue, two early 1900s redbrick buildings are seated side by side in a historic district that was just made richer by the addition of a little grocery store building.

TINY STEPS TOWARD BIG THINGS

These grandiose projects we've taken on have only grown in scale. If we knew how long the Leluia Hall renovation project was going to take in the 1915 church building, I don't think we would have done it. It took a full three years. I guess that's the blessing of not knowing the future. This effort was a terribly trying project that required us to keep our eyes steadfast on what we wanted to do and take even the tiniest of steps each day to move toward it.

Many times more than I'd like to confess, those "tiny steps" were just walking into the building to say hello to our foreman, Dalton. For nearly the whole first year, the room looked the same from when we had gotten it—tight brown carpet, beige walls, double columns holding up the mezzanine.

Slowly the room transformed as we ripped up the flooring to find a black-and-white checkered tile that sat atop a slanted floor that used to lead churchgoers to the front pulpit—layers of time peeled up by hammers and levers. As time inched along, steel beams arrived to secure the structure, and large trusses were raised high along the interior sides of the building.

Each week, I'd walk in again to see little progress made—just a dusty room with a near-empty table where Dalton continued to sit, waiting for when it was time . . . "go time." It was far from "go time."

But eventually, as we rounded into the end of year three, paint went up and wallpaper got rolled out. Lighting fixtures were put in place. Tile covered the bathroom walls. The beautiful touches we had picked out a couple years before were finally installed.

I don't know if pushing harder would have helped. Maybe. But during the "wait," we did some big things. And as much as it took a long time, I imagine by the Universe's standards that it took exactly the right amount of time. Everything aligned just so: We had a more robust, talented team. Our kids got a couple more successful, healthy years in while we tended to the project. We found new projects for our pipeline. We began filming for the PBS show—something that surely benefited from getting a comprehensive look at a full-scale restaurant buildout (more on this later).

Six weeks before opening, everything buzzed to life. That's how it always is. There's all this waiting time, and then suddenly, there's a gigantic push to finish it all up. In time, as everyone did their parts, the room began to clear out, clean up, and get ready for furniture. And that's when the next phase begins, pulling in the team for training—the team who Jeff and I would eventually have to pass the whole project off to. After three years of heartache, frustration, work, vision—just like all the other projects—it comes time to let it go, to pass it off.

Beyond Leluia Hall and the Leeper-Wyatt building, our efforts extend to a third project as well. We've purchased an ugly, flat-top industrial space in the busy South End area where we will put a commissary. This commissary will be where our team makes cocktail syrups and broths; we'll do butchery and bread baking and pasta making. We'll also make the commissary kitchen completely shoppable so that guests can come and get the homemade products we make for our restaurants and take them home to enjoy. It's a similar concept to the Lego model we built—just in a different building, in a different neighborhood, with a different setup, and several years later. I imagine this project, like the others, will be a series of tiny steps that make you feel like you're getting nowhere, but over the course of the year, something beautiful is brought to life.

Every small step matters. I've looked back at some of our buildout lists, and they are astounding. There are lists a dozen bullets long under each of these categories from decor, lighting, and table tops to the menu, training, sourcing, and opening events. But small steps forward matter a lot. They stack one on top of the next, and over time, you look around at a world you hardly recognize.

IT'S SHOWTIME

As we walk forward into the opening of these three additional concepts— Leluia Hall, the Leeper-Wyatt building (concept to be determined!), and our commissary—we're also stepping into new territory personally, too, and it's not like anything we've experienced before.

Our hands were clasped, Jeff's and mine. It was broad daylight, and we were walking down a busy street in Logroño, Spain. It should have felt normal, but it didn't. At all. Large black camera lenses traced our steps, our gaze, our every movement. We walked forward. My breath was quick, and I worked to slow it. People stared at us, and I feigned I didn't notice. Inside—over and over again—I coerced my mind to center. It was not a centering moment; it was a moment of overwhelm—until I remembered that it is in the center of the storm where it is most calm. *Channel the eye of the storm, Jamie.*

We had started filming for our PBS television show, *Fork & Hammer*, and while we had begun filming weeks before, *this* was the first time we were filming in public. People could see us. They didn't know who we were. They shouldn't know who we were. They just watched, whispering, wondering who this couple was and why cameras were following them. "They must be someone," I imagined they were saying, and I had no way of explaining that we weren't and we were doing something and it didn't exist yet. We pretended to be filmworthy when we were just, well, us.

We ate a rich, savory potato "tortilla" in a window reserved for us in San Sebastián, with cameras on multiple sides, zooming in on the steam, the golden richness, the potato layers—and a line down the street with people waiting to get one of those tortillas. That was me in that line for the first forty-six years of my life. Jeff and I would have gotten in line early in the morning for that special dish because we would have read somewhere in some place that it was one of the "it" things to do. Now I had my own torte reserved for me in a window.

After sorting through occasional exhaustion and the discomfort of filming in public, Jeff and I got pretty used to it all. Our restaurant team did too. They stepped into the opportunity much more easily than I expected. We had had some TV opportunities come and go over the years, and it was like I was the one who needed to grow and "get there." Our teammates seemed to have been ready for it all along.

We got lucky with an incredible production team with a lot of synergies. The production company, Susie Films, dives in. So do we. They think bigger than where they are. So do we. They find spots where they're weak, and they fill those in with someone great. So do we. They see potential uplift, beauty, and inspiration in a difficult business. So do we. And we're both masters of the edit. In making restaurants and making television entertainment, it's all about editing. Iteration upon iteration is what finally delivers a great experience.

But here's the thing: I don't know how all this is going to go—these are bold steps, and there's still uncertainty. It's completely new for us. I have unsure feelings about the future, what having a television program will mean, and how it might change my life. I'm happy where I am, and stepping forward into something big like this means change, new challenges, and unknown circumstances. I'll have situations ahead of me that I've never navigated. That's the challenging part of growth—it's a little scary, you're a little vulnerable, and perhaps naively hopeful that the gigantic wave will feel thrilling and not pull you to the bottom of the sea. So I go back to the beginning. I close my eyes. I scoot all those worries aside. I see the vision of a joyful, fun, vibrant, uplifting road ahead—I build on that belief. And despite all those worries, we go anyway.

Fork & Hammer hit screens in October 2025, a ten-part series on public television. It brought on new feelings, new opportunities, and still higher expectations of ourselves. It was a chance to show a small glimpse into our world and the tremendous effort and joy and passion that gets put into every restaurant we have—not just from us, but from our team, hundreds strong.

Being content where you are is a beautiful thing. Wanting to grow is also a beautiful thing. For Jeff and me, we are content staying right where we are in a growth mindset. It carries its share of uncertainty, and it requires a great deal of trust in the world around us, but that mindset brings about a richer, fuller life as we march into the future.

SERVING SPOON: What's your long-term dream (you know, the big one that lights you up), and what steps can you take—no matter how small—to help you move toward it?

CONCLUSION

I never imagined I could be there, and as we approached, the place was nothing like I'd expected. The entrance, completely hidden from view, was tucked down a narrow outdoor corridor with vines and flowers marking the way. Homey and built of wood and stone, I wondered how a fairly nondescript building could become one of the most famous restaurants in the world: The French Laundry.

Since we showed up early for our reservation, we were encouraged to enjoy time in the gardens across the street. My photo-finger wouldn't stop. Grassy paths split raised gardens sprouting kale, tomatoes, edible flowers, and herbs; sunlight streamed down in rays, hazy and golden; a chicken coop with beautiful, black-feathered chickens was a-squawk with chattering hens; in the greenhouse were rows and rows of delicate microgreens making their ways up from the dark, rich soil. Colors—green, white, and yellow drops—shined under a radically blue California sky.

When it was time, we made our way to the host stand, proud to dine in a place of wonder. We were seated upstairs in a private room that was smaller than I'd expected. The round table was snug with chairs and full place settings in a tight, intimate space with an open balcony and fresh air. Jeff and I and the rest of our group lined up for a photo on our balcony with a champagne toast to celebrate the evening. As our executive chef at Supperland, Chris, a large man, rose from the table with his champagne glass in hand, his shoulder hit the sconce on the wall, which fell and shattered. Heads turned abruptly—accidents did not happen at The French Laundry. *Did we all not belong in this place?*

There, in a room of idols and dreams, something broke. But our anxieties were misplaced. Within minutes, the sconce was swept up, and an entirely new sconce replaced it. Apparently, we weren't the first to break something, and I wondered how many other people had felt unworthy, even briefly, only to be rescued by magical healing as a new sconce rose to the wall. We could laugh. We were welcome. We belonged after all. After a tour of their pristine kitchens and floor-to-ceiling wine collection, the night's dreaminess eventually came to a close. Our time at The French Laundry was up. But something stirred within.

Being around the best opens your eyes to becoming your best too. That's been true for Jeff and me. Traveling and experiencing the world provides great inspiration for us. We collect details to incorporate into our business and make improvements. But the single greatest "data point" can never be harnessed or captured: the *feeling* a place gives you. That uncontainable, elusive feeling lifts you from one state to a higher place.

We didn't start as the best. Far from it. What it takes to be multistar Michelin places and Top Restaurants in the World, well, that's probably not a feat we'll aim for. To us, these restaurants we have and this growing restaurant family is perfect. And it's not perfect in that it's flawless, but it's perfect in that it's an intricately connected web of people, partners, guests, experiences, dreams, hopes, creativity, passion, and belief.

We love what we do. Jeff and I take the time, thought, energy, and patience to build restaurants because we love making interesting places for people to enjoy. We invite fun and happiness into our dining experiences—elements that are both difficult to define and subjective—and that invitation has been a difference-maker in the success of our business. People come to our restaurants to eat, but they come in equal part for the feelings that our eating spots give. We bring magic and life to a space through connections of love and gratitude, experiences and beauty, and memories and joy—and those connections blossom with the flavors and experiences of food and drink. Dozens of tactics and strategies have been imperative to our success. Some are numerical understandings, some super soft, some are experiences that life taught us along the way. But still, there's that one secret ingredient pervading all of it: *belief.*

We don't step forward into something new unless we believe we can. We don't let go of responsibility unless we believe in those around us. We don't take risks, have patience, overcome fears, evolve, and adapt without belief. With belief, we have a willingness to expect more of ourselves, our business, and our direction. With belief, we are limitless.

Belief in whatever we're doing makes us jump enthusiastically into projects despite trepidation and uncertainty. Belief lights the way when the road is murky and unclear. Belief, by some unknown process conducted by the powers that be, spurs desirous events to move nearer. Belief brings about uncanny patience because we know, each day, we're taking one more step, and eventually those steps will add up, and we'll be right where we'd hoped. Belief carries with it a magic that glues millions of tiny pieces together to make something new.

Anything that doesn't exist, that comes to life, begins with a thought of what could be. We see it before it's there to see, and we drive forward with boldness, to solve problems, to negotiate successfully, to sign a lease, to start a menu draft—all of it. Big dreams don't come true overnight, but over many working days, capped by dream-filled nights—all as the building blocks stack, one on top of the other, an entire wall is built, then a room, then a full-scale restaurant. Each day we chisel away at the master-piece, and it slowly morphs into what we imagined. We started with eleven tables—and one plate at a time, enjoyed one bite at a time, originating from one ingredient at a time.

There are countless reasons to release a dream and let it float away. It's easier, perhaps more logical, and it might even be more fruitful financially. But maybe you're here on earth to do something beautiful, to create. Maybe you came to play and risk and make an impact. You only need one reason to go after your dream: It lights you up. And you only need one person's permission—yours.

RECIPES

On the following pages, I've included several simple recipes that pertain to some of the food items I mention in the book. I've selected items that can be used at home easily; they can serve as a base for cooking, and they'll cross over in your kitchen flexibly.

I want to thank our chefs for sharing these recipes—Chef Steve Kuney, Chef Chris Rogienski, Chef Sam Sheehan, Pastry Chef Savannah Foltz, and Mixologist Colleen Hughes.

Hopefully, even if you live really far away from us, you'll get a little taste of our world.

EVER ANDALO HOMEMADE PASTA

SERVES 6

This homemade pasta recipe comes from our Italian restaurant, Ever Andalo. It's simple and gives you a starting point for any number of dishes like Bolognese, carbonara, simple tomato sauce, or an olive oil with fresh herbs.

INGREDIENTS:

5 eggs
3½ cups (434 grams) Doppio Zero flour
Extra flour (for work surfaces)
Semolina flour (for dusting)

1. In a medium-sized mixing bowl, whisk eggs until smooth.

2. In a stand mixer equipped with a dough hook, add the flour and gradually add the whisked eggs. Mix until dough is incorporated, with the eggs and flour smoothly blended, creating a large dough ball. Transfer to a work area dusted with extra flour and continue to knead the dough by hand until it's smooth and the flour is fully combined. Wrap in plastic and let sit for at least 30 minutes.

3. Press the dough out and, with a rolling pin, roll until about an inch thick.

4. Set up a stand mixer with a pasta roller and adjust to the largest setting. Flour the roller and pass the dough through, catching it with your other hand. Fold the dough over and repeat this step on the same thickness setting twice.

5. Continue to pass the dough through the roller, reducing the thickness by one notch each time until you reach number 3 or your desired thickness.

6. Lay the dough on a freshly floured workspace and cut sheets into your desired length, usually 8 to 12 inches long.

7. Set up a mixer with a pasta cutter attachment and gently pass sheets through the attachment, catching them with your other hand as they emerge below. Hang the cut pasta on a pasta drying rack and let sit for 20 minutes.

8. Form pasta into nests and place on a parchment-lined sheet tray dusted with semolina flour.

9. Place in boiling water for 3 to 4 minutes, testing for al dente doneness.

10. Enjoy with your favorite sauce, olive oil, or grated cheese.

CRÊPE CELLAR SAVORY CRÊPE BATTER

SERVES 6

This is the crêpe batter recipe we used at our first restaurant, Crêpe Cellar. It's a versatile savory crêpe batter that makes for a delicious base to hold meats, cheeses, or vegetables.

INGREDIENTS:

3 eggs

1 cup whole milk

½ cup water

1 cup all-purpose flour

⅓ cup buckwheat flour

1 teaspoon kosher salt

5 tablespoons melted butter (plus 1 tablespoon additional to coat the pan)

1. Whisk the eggs, milk, and water in a large mixing bowl. Add both flours and the salt. Whisk until smooth.

2. Add the melted butter and whisk until no lumps remain and the batter is smooth.

3. Heat a medium nonstick pan or crêpe griddle over medium heat and add 1 tablespoon of butter to coat the pan.

4. Add ½ cup of the batter to the pan and swirl it around to cover the pan. For a smaller pan, simply use a smaller amount of batter. Cook until the top of the crêpe is firm and no longer liquid.

5. Using a nonstick spatula, gently flip the crêpe and cook for an additional 1 minute.

6. Remove from the pan, fold into a half-moon, and set aside. Repeat the procedure with the remaining batter, a half cup at a time.

7. Crêpes may be filled with a variety of different fillings, like a mix of different cheeses, steak with onions, or grilled chicken and sautéed vegetables.

SUPPERLAND BLACKENED ONIONS
MAKES 1 QUART

Blackened onions are one of our mainstay dishes at our steakhouse concept, Supperland. The dish originates in our home kitchen, as I used it as a major flavor component for my food when I was on an elimination diet. With just three ingredients, it's simple—and it can be enjoyed on a burger, over tacos, mixed into a sauce for pasta, or on a favorite bread.

INGREDIENTS:

4 medium-sized Vidalia onions
2 cups extra virgin olive oil
2 to 2½ teaspoons Maldon salt (or salt to taste)

1. Preheat oven to 450°F.

2. Peel onions and remove the top and root. Slice in half (from top to bottom root). Then slice onions into strips about ¼- to ½-inch wide (at their widest point).

3. Place onions in a 10-inch oven-safe pot and separate the onion layers so the points are sticking up in the pot. It should look pretty packed. (More onion points sticking up will give you a more blackened dish.)

4. Pour olive oil over the onions—the olive oil should rise about one-third of the way up your standing onions.

5. Sprinkle the salt evenly over the top.

6. Bake onions for 30 minutes, allowing the tips to blacken. Depending on your oven and if you want more blackening, simply continue baking for another 10 to 15 minutes.

7. Drop the temperature of the oven to 325°F and allow to slow-cook for 70 to 80 minutes. The onions will get meltier over time and can be left to cook for up to two hours.

8. Serve with meats, bread, rice, or mixed into a pasta dish.

SEAFOOD BALSAMIC MIGNONETTE
MAKES ABOUT 1¾ CUPS

Jeff and I enjoy petite oysters. We love Beausoleils and pink ladies, or a southern favorite, Dukes of Topsail, as examples. This mignonette—which we've used across several concepts for different dishes—has been delicious to enjoy with any oyster varietals, and it's also a great mignonette for grilled fish.

INGREDIENTS:

Zest of a half lemon
1 tablespoon finely chopped Italian parsley
1 tablespoon finely chopped cilantro
½ serrano pepper, seeds removed, finely diced
1 tablespoon finely diced shallots
1 cup white balsamic vinegar
2 teaspoons granulated sugar

1. Add the lemon zest to a mixing bowl.

2. Add remaining ingredients and whisk well to combine. Spoon over your favorite shucked raw oysters or grilled seafood.

EVER ANDALO RICOTTA
SERVES 6

Homemade ricotta is a staple at Ever Andalo, where we serve it topped with toasted pistachios, honey, and a sprinkle of colorful flower petals, alongside our fresh-baked focaccia bread. Ricotta also garnishes a couple of our pasta dishes, adding a fresh touch, and it is excellent as a rich layer in a homemade lasagna.

INGREDIENTS:

8 cups whole milk
2 cups heavy cream
2 teaspoons kosher salt
⅓ cup lemon juice
Salt to taste

1. Place milk, cream, and salt in a nonreactive pot (stainless steel, glass, glazed ceramic, or enamelware) and heat to 195°F, stirring to avoid scorching. Do not boil, as the mixture will become grainy.

2. Add lemon juice, give mixture one stir, and remove from the heat.

3. Let mixture sit for 5 minutes to allow the cream to curdle.

4. Line a large fine mesh strainer with cheesecloth over another pot and slowly strain the liquid whey from the mixture. Do not press the mixture through the strainer.

5. Allow the mixture to sit in the strainer for 20 minutes (for a light and fluffy consistency) to 1 hour (for a firmer consistency).

6. Scoop out your ricotta from the cheese cloth, salt to taste, and enjoy.

Side note: We use the run-off whey (the liquid strained off from the cheese curds) to brine our whole chickens for our Chicken Piccata dish at Ever Andalo.

SUPPERLAND'S SIGNATURE GIANT CHOCOLATE CHIP COOKIES
MAKES 6 LARGE COOKIES

We have a bag of four giant cookies available for take-away at Supperland. After finishing dinner, guests can purchase a bag to enjoy at home. While we love our large, over-the-top treats, you can portion the batter to make smaller cookies if you prefer.

INGREDIENTS:

¾ cup chopped pecans

6 tablespoons benne seeds*

3¼ cups all-purpose flour

¼ cup cornstarch

1 teaspoon Morton's kosher salt

1 teaspoon baking soda

½ pound (2 sticks) butter, softened

⅔ cup sugar

⅔ cup packed light brown sugar

2 eggs

1 egg yolk

1 cup semi-sweet or dark chocolate chips

1. Preheat your oven to 350°F. Meanwhile, prepare a cookie sheet by lining it with parchment paper.

2. Toast the pecans and benne seeds: Place pecans and benne seeds on two separate baking sheets. In the preheated oven, toast seeds and nuts for 5 minutes. Allow to cool fully before making your cookie dough.

3. Make your cookie dough: Preheat oven to 375°F. In a bowl, combine flour, cornstarch, salt, baking soda, and toasted benne seeds. Set these dry ingredients aside until ready to use.

4. In the bowl of a stand mixer (or a mixing bowl, if using a hand mixer) combine butter, sugar, and brown sugar. Use a paddle attachment to cream the butter with the sugars until the mixture is light in color, approximately 2 to 5 minutes. Despite having brown sugar, this mixture should be nearly white when it is properly creamed.

5. Use a spatula to scrape down the sides of your bowl to ensure everything will be properly mixed together. Add eggs and egg yolk to creamed butter and sugar, and continue mixing until everything is well combined and no longer looks "chunky."

6. Again, scrape down the sides of your bowl. Add the set-aside dry ingredients. Mix until just barely combined. At this time, the dough should look crumbly, maybe even with a pocket or two of flour, and not fully mixed together.

7. Add chocolate and toasted pecans, and continue mixing the dough until the chocolate and nuts are evenly distributed throughout.

8. If using a scale, portion your cookies into 5-ounce cookie balls. Otherwise, you can portion them to be approximately ¾ cup each.** Round each portion into a ball, and then slightly flatten it so that the shape resembles a hockey puck.

9. Place 4 to 6 well-spaced cookies onto each tray.

10. Bake the cookies for 8 minutes.

11. After 8 minutes, rotate the cookie sheet so that the cookies that were at the back of the oven are now toward the front. Change the oven temperature to 365°F (no need to re-preheat, just keep rolling!) and bake for another 10 minutes.

12. Allow to cool before removing cookies from the cookie sheet.

This recipe works even better if you make the dough a day before and store it in the refrigerator overnight to allow the flour to hydrate.

*If you are unable to find benne seeds, they can be replaced easily with sesame seeds for a slightly different flavor, or they can be omitted.

** If you desire smaller cookies, you can portion these as small as you would like—you'll just need to cut back the time and possibly the temperature, depending on your oven. For 1-ounce cookies, bake them at 350°F for 8 minutes.

SUPPERLAND AMBROSIA SALAD

SERVES 6

Here in the south, marshmallow dishes are easily served as a side at supper. This ambrosia salad recipe from Supperland takes a classic recipe and elevates it with heavy cream, fresh fruit, candied pecans, and fresh-toasted coconut. It's the gold standard for ambrosia salad.

INGREDIENTS:

1 cup brown sugar

1 cup water

1 cup frozen dark cherries

¼ cup brandy of your choice

1 cup candied pecans

½ cup shredded coconut

½ cup mini marshmallows

½ cup diced pineapple

8 ounces cream cheese

⅓ cup powdered sugar

1 cup heavy cream

1. Combine brown sugar and water in a saucepot and bring to a boil. Whisk until smooth.

2. Place cherries in a small bowl. Pour sugar mixture over cherries. Add brandy. Allow to cool.

3. In a separate bowl, mix the pecans, coconut, marshmallows, and pineapple together and set aside.

4. In a mixing bowl, mix the cream cheese and powdered sugar until no lumps remain.

5. In a stand mixer, whip the heavy cream until stiff peaks form. Fold

whipped cream into the cream cheese mixture, one-third at a time, until smooth. Set aside.

6. In dessert cups, layer the whipped cream, then the pecan/pineapple mixture, and the cherries last.

7. Serve fresh for best results, but the dessert can sit covered in the fridge up to a day before your event.

CRÊPE CELLAR / GROWLERS POURHOUSE PESTO

YIELDS 1 PINT

For many years, one of our most well-loved dishes at Crêpe Cellar was our Pesto Brie Fries. Imagine a large plate of hot, hand-cut, twice-fried french fries topped with pesto, Brie cheese, and fresh tomatoes. With Crêpe Cellar no longer being in operation, we serve the Pesto Brie Fries at Growlers Pourhouse—plus, we've used this pesto at Ever Andalo over vegetable sides and entrée specials.

INGREDIENTS:

½ cup hand-grated Parmigiano Reggiano

8 ounces basil leaves, stems removed

½ cup pine nuts

1 tablespoon minced garlic

6 ounces (¾ cup) extra virgin olive oil

1 tablespoon water

½ teaspoon salt or to taste

1. Place Parmigiano, basil, pine nuts, and garlic in a food processor equipped with an S-blade and puree until well chopped and combined.

2. Slowly add olive oil to the running food processor and process until smooth. Adjust consistency with water and adjust seasoning with salt.

GRAIN-FREE BANANA MUFFINS WITH OPTIONAL VEGAN ICING

12 MUFFINS

This is my personal allergen-friendly banana muffin recipe. I keep these muffins on hand every week. Typically, I enjoy them with coconut oil once baked, but I've included a delicious allergen-friendly, vegan frosting recipe that we use at Reigning Doughnuts if you want to make this muffin a sweeter treat.

MUFFIN INGREDIENTS:

1 cup cassava flour

½ cup tiger nut flour (tiger nut is a tuber, not a nut!)

½ teaspoon Maldon salt

1 teaspoon baking soda

3½ large overripe bananas, smashed

2 eggs

4 tablespoons maple syrup (you can cut this back to about 2 tablespoons to keep sugar down)

1 teaspoon vanilla

½ cup water

4 teaspoons apple cider vinegar

¾ cup avocado oil

1. Preheat oven to 350°F. Spray a 12-cup muffin pan with nonstick cooking spray or line with muffin liners.

2. Whisk both flours, salt, and baking soda together until well combined.

3. In a separate bowl, smash the bananas to your liking. It's okay to have some larger pieces. Then add the eggs, syrup, vanilla, water, and vinegar to the bananas. Mix well.

4. Combine the dry ingredients with the wet ingredients and mix until just combined, keeping some banana chunks whole and not over-mixing. Divide the mix evenly into the prepared muffin cups.

5. Bake for 28 minutes. Allow to cool 5 minutes in the pan and then move the muffins to a cooling rack. Serve with coconut oil, butter, or icing.

REIGNING DOUGHNUTS VEGAN, ALLERGEN-FRIENDLY ICING INGREDIENTS:

2 cups palm shortening

¼ cup tapioca flour

1 cup date sugar

4 teaspoons vanilla extract

½ teaspoon salt

1. Combine all ingredients into a stand mixer bowl. Mix until a smooth and creamy consistency is achieved.

2. Top your muffins using a knife or piping bag.

HABERDISH MINT JULEP
PARTY SIZE!

The Mint Julep is one of our flagship cocktails at Haberdish. We serve the drink in a copper julep cup with a generous fresh mint garnish. Syrup makes enough for up to 15 cocktails for an at-home cocktail party. Directions below are for a single drink.

MINT SYRUP INGREDIENTS
(SYRUP RECIPE TO MAKE 15 DRINKS):

1½ cups water
1 cup white sugar
2 ounces fresh mint
Pinch of salt (to taste)

1. In a saucepot, bring water and sugar to a low boil.

2. Reduce to a simmer and add the mint. Simmer for 10 minutes.

3. Cool and then strain out the mint leaves. Set aside to mix into your julep.

MINT JULEP COCKTAIL INGREDIENTS (MAKES ONE DRINK):

Mint leaves
Crushed ice
1½ ounces mint syrup
2 ounces bourbon

1. Gently muddle a few mint leaves in a glass.

2. Add the ice, mint syrup, and bourbon.

3. Lightly stir to combine.

4. Top with more crushed ice, a big sprig of mint, and a straw.

ACKNOWLEDGMENTS

A number of people are due recognition in helping to complete this book. First, my children. Watching them grow into thoughtful, responsible people with big dreams brings meaning to everything Jeff and I build. Isabella, Eli, and Isaac, you are part of everything we create. Your presence on this journey brings greater purpose to all the work we do. Thank you for walking beside us and inspiring us.

Gratitude goes out to Maya Myers, a very early editor—thank you for helping shape the initial stages of this project with your insight and encouragement. You got it to a place where I felt good about carrying it forward. I'd also like to thank the supportive editorial, design, and project management team at Greenleaf Book Group: Jen Glynn, Pam Norberg, Fallon Clark, Mimi Bark, and especially Sally Garland—thank you for your thoughtful guidance, care, and commitment to bringing this book to life.

Many years ago I wrote a book that I self-published but never went any further with. There were many people who helped me with that project, and I never got to formerly thank them with a successful published piece. Thank you for your belief in me and for encouraging me to keep writing: Holly Patterson, Tyler Epp, Kristen Loughmiller, Nancy Brown, Joyce Hollyday, Darla Bruno, Sheila Dunn Kley, Kerry Brown, and Harla Brown. I couldn't have finished that book without you, and with your support, I've continued my love for writing.

To both my parents, for their kind, steady support—and to my mom, for reading early versions of *Eleven Tables* with care and interest. To my identical twin sister, Kerry, for being an early reader of this work, as well as a lifelong cheerleader. Not many people are gifted a best friend at birth—and I'm so grateful for how we're always pushing each other toward greater things.

I wish to thank our restaurant investors—people who stepped up and believed in us before anything real could be seen. Whether a large-scale church–restaurant renovation or a meager eleven-table eatery, we couldn't dream big without the financial support of others. It's because of you that we've been able to create unique dining spots. Thank you for betting on us.

To our restaurant team—thank you. What a gift it is to work alongside you. While we currently have 300 team members, we've had the privilege of employing thousands over the years. I'm deeply grateful to each person who has helped us serve delicious food and warm hospitality to the city of Charlotte. To our chefs and managers: Lindsey Robbins, Allie Papajohn, Chris Rogienski, Jon Rosenberg, Joe Hutton, Sam Sheehan, Lex Farlardeau, Savannah Foltz, Cortney Gutowski, Harry Ewell, Moriah Glenn, Katie Thompson, and Bry Keogh—you hold these places together. You are the reason we can keep building. Thank you. Your commitment is the heartbeat of what we do.

Last, I thank my husband, Jeff—this dream began with your belief. You had the boldness to start, the steadiness to sustain, and the vision to grow something meaningful. Your creativity, courage, and unwavering partnership have shaped everything this book stands for. You have lifted me when I was weak, and encouraged me still higher when I was strong. Though these are my words, this is our story.

ABOUT THE AUTHOR

JAMIE BROWN is the owner of the Tonidandel-Brown Restaurant Group, along with her husband, Jeff Tonidandel. The couple currently owns and operates six of Charlotte, North Carolina's, most celebrated dining spots, including Ever Andalo, Growlers Pourhouse, Haberdish, Leluia Hall, Reigning Doughnuts, and Supperland (*"Bon Appétit's* 10 Best New Restaurants in the US 2022"*).

The Tonidandel-Brown Restaurant Group has a strong focus on adaptive reuse projects for their hospitality concepts, along with creating unique handcrafted touches for the dining environment, designed and constructed by their team. Known for developing a culture of love and growth, their independent restaurant business has grown more than 25 percent a year for the last fifteen years. With more restaurant concepts on the way, their business growth story, approach to creating restaurants, and development of a culinary team is featured in the PBS series *Fork & Hammer*. Jamie and Jeff have three children, Isabella, Eli, and Isaac.